The Mabi

(Volume 2)

Editor: Owen Morgan Edwards

(Translator: Lady Charlotte Schreiber)

Alpha Editions

This edition published in 2022

ISBN : 9789356576599

Design and Setting By
Alpha Editions
www.alphaedis.com
Email - info@alphaedis.com

Contents

INTRODUCTION.

In this second volume, as in the first, I have given Lady Charlotte Guest's translation exactly as she wrote it. It would have been easy to make it a more faithful reproduction of the Welsh by occasionally changing a word, or by making a phrase more simple in diction. But the reader would not have forgiven me for placing before him a translation that was not Lady Charlotte Guest's. I have again ventured, however, after a careful comparison of the translation with the original, to put in the form of footnotes a more accurate or more literal rendering of passages which Lady Charlotte Guest did not read aright, passages which she has omitted, and passages the real meaning of which she seems to me to have failed to grasp.

The first two tales in this volume make up, with "The Dream of Rhonabwy," the second volume of the original edition. "The Dream of Rhonabwy" was placed in my first volume, with "The Lady of the Fountain" and "Peredur"— the two tales that form the first volume of the original edition. The oldest of the tales—the Mabinogion proper—will all be included in the third volume.

OWEN EDWARDS.

LLANUWCHLLYN,
June 1902.

GERAINT THE SON OF ERBIN.

Arthur was accustomed to hold his Court at Caerlleon upon Usk. And there he held it seven Easters, [7a] and five Christmases. And once upon a time he held his Court there at Whitsuntide. For Caerlleon was the place most easy of access in his dominions, both by sea and by land. And there were assembled [7b] nine crowned kings, who were his tributaries, and likewise earls and barons. For they were his invited guests at all the high festivals, unless they were prevented by any great hindrance. And when he was at Caerlleon, holding his Court, thirteen churches were set apart for mass. And thus were they appointed: one church for Arthur, and his kings, and his guests; and the second for Gwenhwyvar and her ladies; and the third for the Steward of the Household and the Suitors; and the fourth for the Franks, and the other officers; and the other nine churches were for the nine Masters of the Household, and chiefly for Gwalchmai; for he, from the eminence of his warlike fame, and from the nobleness of his birth, was the most exalted of the nine. And there was no other arrangement respecting the churches than that which we have mentioned above.

Glewlwyd Gavaelvawr was the chief porter; but he did not himself perform the office, except at one of the three high festivals, for he had seven men to serve him; and they divided the year amongst them. They were Grynn, and

Pen Pighon, and Llaes Cymyn, and Gogyfwlch, and Gwrdnei with Cat's eyes, who could see as well by night as by day, and Drem the son of Dremhitid, and Clust the son of Clustveinyd; and these were Arthur's guards. And on Whit Tuesday, as the King sat at the banquet, lo! there entered a tall, fair-headed youth, clad in a coat and a surcoat of diapred satin, and a golden-hilted sword about his neck, and low shoes of leather upon his feet. And he came, and stood before Arthur. "Hail to thee, Lord!" said he. "Heaven prosper thee," he answered, "and be thou welcome. Dost thou bring any new tidings?" "I do, Lord," he said. "I know thee not," said Arthur. "It is a marvel to me that thou dost not know me. I am one of thy foresters, Lord, in the Forest of Dean, and my name is Madawc, the son of Twrgadarn." "Tell me thine errand," said Arthur. "I will do so, Lord," said he. "In the Forest I saw a stag, the like of which beheld I never yet." "What is there about him," asked Arthur, "that thou never yet didst see his like?" "He is of pure white, Lord, and he does not herd with any other animal through stateliness and pride, so royal is his bearing. And I come to seek thy counsel, Lord, and to know thy will concerning him." "It seems best to me," said Arthur, "to go and hunt him to-morrow at break of day; and to cause general notice thereof to be given to-night in all quarters of the Court." And Arryfuerys was Arthur's chief huntsman, and Arelivri was his chief page. And all received notice; and thus it was arranged. And they sent the youth before them. Then Gwenhwyvar said to Arthur, "Wilt thou permit me, Lord," said she, "to go to-morrow to see and hear the hunt of the stag of which the young man spoke?" "I will, gladly," said Arthur. "Then will I go," said she. And Gwalchmai said to Arthur, "Lord, if it seem well to thee, permit that into whose hunt soever the stag shall come, that one, be he a knight or one on foot, may cut off his head, and give it to whom he pleases, whether to his own ladylove, or to the lady of his friend." "I grant it gladly," said Arthur, "and let the Steward of the Household be chastised if all are not ready to-morrow for the chase."

And they passed the night with songs, and diversions, and discourse, and ample entertainment. And when it was time for them all to go to sleep, they went. And when the next day came, they arose; and Arthur called the attendants, who guarded his couch. And these were four pages, whose names were Cadyrnerth the son of Porthawr Gandwy, and Ambreu the son of Bedwor, and Amhar, the son of Arthur, and Goreu the son of Custennin. And these men came to Arthur, and saluted him, and arrayed him in his garments. And Arthur wondered that Gwenhwyvar did not awake, and did not move in her bed: and the attendants wished to awaken her. "Disturb her not," said Arthur, "for she had rather sleep than go to see the hunting."

Then Arthur went forth, and he heard two horns sounding, one from near the lodging of the chief huntsman, and the other from near that of the chief page. And the whole assembly of the multitudes came to Arthur, and they took the road to the Forest.

And after Arthur had gone forth from the palace, Gwenhwyvar awoke, and called to her maidens, and apparelled herself. "Maidens," said she, "I had leave last night to go and see the hunt. Go one of you to the stable, and order hither a horse such as a woman may ride." And one of them went, and she found but two horses in the stable, and Gwenhwyvar and one of her maidens mounted them, and went through the Usk, and followed the track of the men and the horses. And as they rode thus, they heard a loud and rushing sound; and they looked behind them, and beheld a knight upon a [10] hunter foal of mighty size; and the rider was a fair haired youth, bare-legged, and of princely mien, and a golden-hilted sword was at his side, and a robe and a surcoat of satin were upon him, and two low shoes of leather upon his feet; and around him was a scarf of blue purple, at each corner of which was a golden apple. And his horse stepped stately, and swift, and proud; and he overtook Gwenhwyvar, and saluted her. "Heaven prosper thee, Geraint," said she, "I knew thee when first I saw thee just now. And the welcome of heaven be unto thee. And why didst thou not go with thy Lord to hunt?" "Because I knew not when he went," said he. "I marvel too," said she, "how he could go unknown to me." "Indeed, lady," said he. "I was fast asleep, and knew not when he went; but thou, O young man, art the most agreeable companion I could have in the whole kingdom; and it may be that I shall be more amused with the hunting than they; [11] for we shall hear the horns when they sound, and we shall hear the dogs when they are let loose, and begin to cry." So they went to the edge of the Forest, and there they stood. "From this place," said she, "we shall hear when the dogs are let loose." And thereupon they heard a loud noise, and they looked towards the spot whence it came, and they beheld a dwarf riding upon a horse, stately, and foaming, and prancing, and strong, and spirited. And in the hand of the dwarf was a whip. And near the dwarf they saw a lady upon a beautiful white horse, of steady and stately pace; and she was clothed in a garment of gold brocade. And near her was a knight upon a war-horse of large size, with heavy and bright armour both upon himself and upon his horse. And truly they never before saw a knight, or a horse, or armour, of such remarkable size. And they were all near to each other.

"Geraint," said Gwenhwyvar, "knowest thou the name of that tall knight yonder?" "I know him not," said he, "and the strange armour that he wears prevents my either seeing his face or his features." "Go, maiden," said Gwenhwyvar, "and ask the dwarf who that knight is." Then the maiden went up to the dwarf; and the dwarf waited for the maiden, when he saw her coming towards him. And the maiden enquired of the dwarf who the knight was. "I will not tell thee," he answered. "Since thou art so churlish as not to tell me," said she, "I will ask him himself." "Thou shall not ask him, by my faith," said he. "Wherefore?" said she. "Because thou art not of honour sufficient to befit thee to speak to my Lord." Then the maiden turned her horse's head towards the knight, upon which the dwarf struck her with the whip that was in his hand across the face and the eyes, until the blood flowed forth. And the maiden, through the hurt she received from the blow, returned to Gwenhwyvar, complaining of the pain. "Very rudely has the dwarf treated thee," said Geraint. "I will go myself to know who the knight is." "Go," said Gwenhwyvar. And Geraint went up to the dwarf. "Who is yonder knight?" said Geraint. "I will not tell thee," said the dwarf. "Then will I ask him himself," said he. "That wilt thou not, by my faith," said the dwarf; "thou art not honourable enough to speak with my Lord." Said Geraint, "I have spoken with men of equal rank with him." And he turned his horse's head towards the knight, but the dwarf overtook him and struck him as he had done the maiden, so that the blood coloured the scarf that Geraint wore. Then Geraint put his hand upon the hilt of his sword, but he took counsel with himself, and considered that it would be no vengeance for him to slay the dwarf, and to be attacked unarmed by the armed knight, so he returned to where Gwenhwyvar was.

"Thou hast acted wisely and discreetly," said she. "Lady," said he, "I will follow him yet, with thy permission; and at last he will come to some inhabited place, where I may have arms either as a loan or for a pledge, so that I may encounter the knight." "Go," said she, "and do not attack him until thou hast good arms, and I shall be very anxious concerning thee, until I hear tidings of thee." "If I am alive," said he, "thou shall hear tidings of me by to-morrow afternoon;" and with that he departed.

And the road they took was below the palace of Caerlleon, and across the ford of the Usk; and they went along a fair, and even, and lofty ridge of ground, until they came to a town, and at the extremity of the town they saw a Fortress and a Castle. And they came to the extremity of the town. And as the knight passed through it, all the people arose, and saluted him, and bade him welcome. And when Geraint came into the town, he looked at every house, to see if he knew any of those whom he saw. But he knew none, and none knew him to do him the kindness to let him have arms either as a loan or for a pledge. And every house he saw was full of men, and arms, and horses. And they were polishing shields, and burnishing swords, and washing armour, and shoeing horses. And the knight, and the lady, and the dwarf, rode up to the Castle that was in the town, and every one was glad in the Castle. And from the battlements and the gates they risked their necks, through their eagerness to greet them, and to show their joy.

Geraint stood there to see whether the knight would remain in the Castle; and when he was certain that he would do so, he looked around him; and at a little distance from the town he saw an old palace in ruins, wherein was a hall that was falling to decay. And as he knew not any one in the town, he went towards the old palace; and when he came near to the palace, he saw but one chamber, and a bridge of marble-stone leading to it. And upon the bridge he saw sitting a hoary-headed man, upon whom were tattered garments. And Geraint gazed steadfastly upon him for a long time. Then the hoary-headed man spoke to him. "Young man," he said, "wherefore art thou thoughtful?" "I am thoughtful," said he, "because I know not where to go to-night." "Wilt thou come forward this way, chieftain?" said he, "and thou shalt have of the best that can be procured for thee." So Geraint went forward. And the hoary-headed man preceded him into the hall. And in the hall he dismounted, and he left there his horse. Then he went on to the upper chamber with the hoary-headed man. And in the chamber he beheld an old decrepit woman, sitting on a cushion, with old tattered garments of satin upon her; and it seemed to him that he had never seen a woman fairer than she must have been when in the fulness of youth. And beside her was a maiden, upon whom were a vest and a veil, that were old, and beginning to be worn out. And truly he never saw a maiden more full of comeliness, and grace, and beauty, than she. And the hoary-headed man said to the maiden, "There is no attendant for the horse of this youth but thyself." "I will render the best service I am able," said she, "both to him and to his horse." And the maiden disarrayed the youth, and then she furnished his horse with straw and with corn. And she went to the hall as before, and then she returned to the chamber. And the hoary-headed man said to the maiden, "Go to the town," said he, "and bring hither the best that thou canst find both of food and of liquor." "I will, gladly, Lord," said she. And to the town went the maiden. And they conversed together, while the maiden was at the town. And, behold! the maiden came back, and a youth with her, bearing on his back a costrel full of good purchased mead and a quarter of a young bullock. And in the hands of the maiden was a quantity of white bread, and she had some manchet bread in her veil, and she came into the chamber. "I could not obtain better than this," said she, "nor with better should I have been trusted." "It is good enough," said Geraint. And they caused the meat to be boiled; and when their food was ready, they sat down. And it was in this wise; Geraint sat between the hoary-headed man and his wife, and the maiden served them. And they ate and drank.

And when they had finished eating, Geraint talked with the hoary-headed man, and he asked him in the first place, to whom belonged the Palace that he was in. "Truly," said he, "it was I that built it, and to me also belonged the city and the castle which thou sawest." "Alas!" said Geraint, "how is it that thou hast lost them now?" "I lost a great Earldom as well as these," said he, "and this is how I lost them. I had a nephew, the son of my brother, and I took his possessions to myself; and when he came to his strength, he demanded of me his property, but I withheld it from him. So he made war upon me, and wrested from me all that I possessed." "Good, Sir," [15] said Geraint, "wilt thou tell me wherefore came the knight, and the lady, and the dwarf, just now into the town, and what is the preparation which I saw, and the putting of arms in order." "I will do so," said he. "The preparations are for the game that is to be held to-morrow by the young Earl, which will be on this wise. In the midst of a meadow which is here, two forks will be set up, and upon the two forks a silver rod, and upon the silver rod a Sparrow-Hawk, and for the Sparrow-Hawk there will be a tournament. And to the tournament will go all the array thou didst see in the city, of men, and of horses, and of arms. And with each man will go the lady he loves best; and no man can joust for the Sparrow-Hawk, except the lady he loves best be with him. And the knight that thou sawest has gained the Sparrow-Hawk these two years; and if he gains it the third year, they will, from that time, send it every year to him, and he himself will come here no more. And he will be called the knight of the Sparrow-Hawk from that time forth." "Sir," said Geraint, "what is thy counsel to me concerning this knight, on account of the insult which I received from the dwarf, and that which was received by the maiden of Gwenhwyvar, the wife of Arthur?" And Geraint told the hoary-headed man what the insult was that he had received. "It is not easy to counsel thee, inasmuch as thou hast neither dame nor maiden belonging to thee, for whom thou canst joust. Yet, I have arms here, which thou couldest have; and there is my horse also, if he seem to thee better than thine own." "Ah! Sir," said he, "Heaven reward thee. But my own horse, to which I am accustomed, together with thine arms, will suffice me. And if, when the appointed time shall come to-morrow, thou wilt permit me, Sir, to challenge for yonder maiden that is thy daughter, I will engage, if I escape from the tournament, to love the maiden as long as I live, and if I do not escape, she will remain unsullied as before." "Gladly will I permit thee," said the hoary-headed man, "and since thou dost thus resolve, it is necessary that thy horse and arms should be ready to-morrow at break of day. For then, the knight of the Sparrow-Hawk will make proclamation, and ask the lady he loves best to take the Sparrow-Hawk. 'For,' will he say to her, 'thou art the fairest of women, and thou didst possess it last year, and the year previous; and if any deny it thee to-day, by force will I defend it for thee.' And therefore," said the hoary-headed man, "it is needful for thee to be there at daybreak; and we three will be with thee," and thus was it settled.

And at night, lo! [17] they went to sleep; and before the dawn they arose, and arrayed themselves; and by the time that it was day, they were all four in the meadow. And there was the knight of the Sparrow-Hawk making the proclamation, and asking his ladylove to fetch the Sparrow-Hawk. "Fetch it not," said Geraint, "for there is here a maiden, who is fairer, and more noble, and more comely, and who has a better claim to it than thou." "If thou maintainest the Sparrow-Hawk to be due to her, come forward, and do battle with me." And Geraint went forward to the top of the meadow, having upon himself and upon his horse armour which was heavy, and rusty, and worthless, and of uncouth shape. Then they encountered each other, and they broke a set of lances, and they broke a second set, and a third. And thus they did at every onset, and they broke as many lances as were brought to them. And when the Earl and his company saw the knight of the Sparrow-Hawk gaining the mastery, there was shouting, and joy, and mirth amongst them. And the hoary-headed man, and his wife, and his daughter, were sorrowful. And the hoary-headed man served Geraint lances as often as he broke them, and the dwarf served the knight of the Sparrow-Hawk. Then the hoary-headed man came to Geraint. "Oh! chieftain," said he, "since no other will hold with thee, behold, here is the lance which was in my hand on the day when I received the honour of knighthood; and from that time to this I never broke it. And it has an excellent point." Then Geraint took the lance, thanking the hoary-headed man. And thereupon the dwarf also brought a lance to his lord. "Behold here is a lance for thee, not less good than his," said the dwarf. "And bethink thee, that no knight ever withstood thee before so long as this one has done." "I declare to Heaven," said Geraint, "that unless death takes me quickly hence, he shall fare never the better for thy service." And Geraint pricked his horse towards him from afar, and warning him, he rushed upon him, and gave him a blow so severe, and furious, and fierce, upon the face of his shield, that he cleft it in two, and broke his armour, and burst his girths, so that both he and his saddle were borne to the ground over the horse's crupper. And Geraint dismounted quickly. And he was wroth, and he drew his sword, and rushed fiercely upon him. Then the knight also arose, and drew his sword against Geraint. And they fought on foot with their swords until their aims struck sparks of fire like stars from one another; and thus they continued fighting until the blood and sweat obscured the light from their eyes. And when Geraint prevailed, the hoary-headed man, and his wife, and his daughter were glad; and when the knight prevailed, it rejoiced the Earl and his party. Then the hoary-headed man saw Geraint receive a severe stroke, and he went up to him quickly, and said to him, "Oh, chieftain, remember the treatment which thou hadst from the dwarf; and wilt thou not seek vengeance for the insult to thyself, and for the insult to Gwenhwyvar the wife of Arthur!" And Geraint was roused by what he said to him, [19] and he called to him all his strength, and lifted up his sword, and struck the knight upon the crown of his head, so that he broke all his head armour, and cut through all the flesh and the skin, even to the skull, until he wounded the bone.

Then the knight fell upon his knees, and cast his sword from his hand, and besought mercy of Geraint. "Of a truth," said he, "I relinquish my overdaring and my pride in craving thy mercy; and unless I have time to commit myself to Heaven for my sins, and to talk with a priest, thy mercy will avail me little." "I will grant thee grace upon this condition," said Geraint, "that thou wilt go to Gwenhwyvar, the wife of Arthur, to do her satisfaction for the insult which her maiden received from thy dwarf. As to myself, for the insult which I received from thee and thy dwarf, I am content with that which I have done unto thee. Dismount not from the time thou goest hence until thou comest into the presence of Gwenhwyvar, to make her what atonement shall be adjudged at the Court of Arthur." "This will I do gladly. And who art thou?" said he. "I am Geraint the son of Erbin. And declare thou also who thou art." "I am Edeyrn the son of Nudd." Then he threw himself upon his horse, and went forward to Arthur's Court, and the lady he loved best went before him and the dwarf, with much lamentation. And thus far this story up to that time.

* * * * *

Then came the little Earl and his hosts to Geraint, and saluted him, and bade him to his castle. "I may not go," said Geraint, "but where I was last night, there will I be to-night also." "Since thou wilt none of my inviting, thou shall have abundance of all that I can command for thee, in the place thou wast last night. And I will order ointment for thee, to recover thee from thy fatigues, and from the weariness that is upon thee." "Heaven reward thee," said Geraint, "and I will go to my lodging." And thus went Geraint, and Earl Ynywl, and his wife, and his daughter. And when they reached the chamber, the household servants and attendants of the young Earl had arrived at the Court, and they arranged all the houses, dressing them with straw and with fire; and in a short time the ointment was ready, and Geraint came there, and they washed his head. Then came the young Earl, with forty honourable knights from among his attendants, and those who were bidden to the tournament. And Geraint came from the anointing. And the Earl asked him to go to the hall to eat. "Where is the Earl Ynywl," said Geraint, "and his wife, and his daughter?" "They are in the chamber yonder," said the Earl's chamberlain, "arraying themselves in garments which the Earl has caused to be brought for them." "Let not the damsel array herself," said he, "except in her vest and her veil, until she come to the Court of Arthur, to be clad by Gwenhwyvar, in such garments as she may choose." So the maiden did not array herself.

Then they all entered the hall, and they washed, and went, and sat down to meat. And thus were they seated. On one side of Geraint sat the young Earl, and Earl Ynywl beyond him; and on the other side of Geraint was the maiden and her mother. And after these all sat according to their precedence in honour. And they ate. And they were served abundantly, and they received a profusion of divers kind of gifts. Then they conversed together. And the young Earl invited Geraint to visit him next day. "I will not, by Heaven," said Geraint. "To the Court of Arthur will I go with this maiden to-morrow. And it is enough for me, as long as Earl Ynywl is in poverty and trouble; and I go chiefly to seek to add to his maintenance." "Ah, chieftain," said the young Earl, "it is not by my fault that Earl Ynywl is without his possessions." "By my faith," said Geraint, "he shall not remain without them, unless death quickly takes me hence." "Oh, chieftain," said he, "with regard to the disagreement between me and Ynywl, I will gladly abide by thy counsel, and agree to what thou mayest judge right between us." [22] "I but ask thee," said Geraint, "to restore to him what is his, and what he should have received from the time he lost his possessions, even until this day." "That will I do gladly, for thee," answered he. "Then," said Geraint, "whosoever is here who owes homage to Ynywl, let him come forward, and perform it on the spot." And all the men did so. And by that treaty they abided. And his castle, and his town, and all his possessions, were restored to Ynywl. And he received back all that he had lost, even to the smallest jewel.

Then spoke Earl Ynywl to Geraint. "Chieftain," said he "behold the maiden for whom thou didst challenge at the tournament, I bestow her upon thee." "She shall go with me," said Geraint, "to the Court of Arthur; and Arthur and Gwenhwyvar, they shall dispose of her as they will." And the next day they proceeded to Arthur's Court. So far concerning Geraint.

* * * * *

Now, this is how Arthur hunted the stag. The men and the dogs were divided into hunting parties, and the dogs were let loose upon the stag. And the last dog that was let loose was the favourite dog of Arthur. Cavall was his name. And he left all the other dogs behind him, and turned the stag. And at the second turn, the stag came towards the hunting party of Arthur. And Arthur set upon him. And before he could be slain by any other, Arthur cut off his head. Then they sounded the death horn for slaying, and they all gathered round.

Then came Kadyrieith to Arthur, and spoke to him. "Lord," said he, "behold yonder is Gwenhwyvar, and none with her save only one maiden." "Command Gildas the son of Caw, and all the scholars of the Court," said Arthur, "to attend Gwenhwyvar to the palace." And they did so.

Then they all set forth, holding converse together concerning the head of the stag, to whom it should be given. One wished that it should be given to the lady best beloved by him, and another to the lady whom he loved best. And all they of the household and the knights disputed sharply concerning the head. And with that they came to the palace. And when Arthur and Gwenhwyvar heard them disputing about the head of the stag, Gwenhwyvar said to Arthur, "My lord, this is my counsel concerning the stag's head; let it not be given away until Geraint the son of Erbin shall return from the errand he is upon." And Gwenhwyvar told Arthur what that errand was. "Right gladly shall it be so," said Arthur. And thus it was settled. And the next day Gwenhwyvar caused a watch to be set upon the ramparts for Geraint's coming. And after mid-day they beheld an unshapely little man upon a horse, and after him, as they supposed, a dame or a damsel, also on horseback, and after her a knight of large stature, bowed down, and hanging his head low and sorrowfully, and clad in broken and worthless armour.

And before they came near to the gate, one of the watch went to Gwenhwyvar, and told her what kind of people they saw, and what aspect they bore. "I know not who they are," said he. "But I know," said Gwenhwyvar, "this is the knight whom Geraint pursued, and methinks that he comes not here by his own free will. But Geraint has overtaken him, and avenged the insult to the maiden to the uttermost." And thereupon, behold a porter came to the spot where Gwenhwyvar was. "Lady," said he, "at the gate there is a knight, and I saw never a man of so pitiful an aspect to look upon as he. Miserable and broken is the armour that he wears, and the hue of blood is more conspicuous upon it than its own colour." "Knowest thou his name?" said she. "I do," said he, "he tells me that he is Edeyrn the son of Nudd." Then she replied, "I know him not."

So Gwenhwyvar went to the gate to meet him, and he entered. And Gwenhwyvar was sorry when she saw the condition he was in, even though he was accompanied by the churlish dwarf. Then Edeyrn saluted Gwenhwyvar. "Heaven protect thee," said she. "Lady," said he, "Geraint the son of Erbin, thy best and most valiant servant, greets thee." "Did he meet with thee?" she asked. "Yes," said he, "and it was not to my advantage; and that was not his fault, but mine, Lady. And Geraint greets thee well; and in greeting thee he compelled me to come hither to do thy pleasure for the insult which thy maiden received from the dwarf. He forgives the insult to himself, in consideration of his having put me in peril of my life. And he imposed on me a condition, manly, and honourable, and warrior-like, which was to do thee justice, Lady." "Now, where did he overtake thee?" "At the place where we were jousting, and contending for the Sparrow-Hawk, in the town which is now called Cardiff. And there were none with him, save three persons, of a mean and tattered condition. And these were an aged, hoary-headed man and a woman advanced in years, and a fair young maiden, clad in worn-out garments. And it was for the avouchment of the love of that maiden that Geraint jousted for the Sparrow-Hawk at the tournament; for he said that that maiden was better entitled to the Sparrow-Hawk than this maiden who was with me. And thereupon we encountered each other, and he left me, Lady, as thou seest." "Sir," said she, "when thinkest thou that Geraint will be here?" "To-morrow, Lady, I think he will be here with the maiden."

Then Arthur came to him, and he saluted Arthur, and Arthur gazed a long time upon him, and was amazed to see him thus. And thinking that he knew him, he enquired of him, "Art thou Edeyrn the son of Nudd?" "I am, Lord," said he, "and I have met with much trouble, and received wounds unsupportable." Then he told Arthur all his adventure.

"Well," said Arthur, "from what I hear, it behoves Gwenhwyvar to be merciful towards thee." "The mercy which thou desirest, Lord," said she, "will I grant to him, since it is as insulting to thee that an insult should be offered to me as to thyself." "Thus will it be best to do," said Arthur, "let this man have medical care until it be known whether he may live. And if he live, he shall do such satisfaction as shall be judged best by the men of the Court; and take thou sureties to that effect. And it he die, too much will be the death of such a youth as Edeyrn for an insult to a maiden." "This pleases me," said Gwenhwyvar. And Arthur became surety for Edeyrn, and

Caradawc the son of Llyr, Gwallawg the son of Llenawg, and Owain the son of Nudd, and Gwalchmai, and many others with them. And Arthur caused Morgan Tud to be called to him. He was the chief physician. "Take with thee Edeyrn the son of Nudd, and cause a chamber to be prepared for him, and let him have the aid of medicine as thou wouldest do unto myself if I were wounded, and let none into his chamber to molest him, but thyself and thy disciples, to administer to him remedies." "I will do so, gladly, Lord," said Morgan Tud. Then said the steward of the household, "Whither is it right, Lord, to order the maiden?" "To Gwenhwyvar and her and maidens," said he. And the Steward of the Household so ordered her. Thus far concerning them.

* * * * *

The next day came Geraint towards the Court, and there was a watch set on the ramparts by Gwenhwyvar, lest he should arrive unawares. And one of the watch came to the place where Gwenhwyvar was. "Lady," said he, "methinks that I see Geraint, and the maiden with him. He is on horseback, but he has his walking gear upon him, and the maiden appears to be in white, seeming to be clad in a garment of linen." "Assemble all the women," said Gwenhwyvar, "and come to meet Geraint, to welcome him, and wish him joy." And Gwenhwyvar went to meet Geraint and the maiden. And when Geraint came to the place where Gwenhwyvar was, he saluted her. "Heaven prosper thee," said she, "and welcome to thee. And thy career has been successful, and fortunate, and resistless, and glorious. And Heaven reward thee, that thou hast so proudly caused me to have retribution." "Lady," said he, "I earnestly desired to obtain thee satisfaction according to thy will; and, behold, here is the maiden through whom thou hadst thy revenge." "Verily," said Gwenhwyvar, "the welcome of Heaven be unto her; and it is fitting that we should receive her joyfully." Then they went in, and dismounted. And Geraint came to where Arthur was, and saluted him. "Heaven protect thee," said Arthur, "and the welcome of Heaven be unto thee. And since [27] Edeyrn the son of Nudd has received his overthrow and wounds from thy hands, thou hadst had a prosperous career." "Not upon me be the blame," said Geraint, "it was through the arrogance of Edeyrn the son of Nudd himself that we were not friends. I would not quit him until I knew who he was, and until the one had vanquished the other." "Now," said Arthur, "where is the maiden for whom I heard thou didst give challenge?" "She is gone with Gwenhwyvar to her chamber." Then went Arthur to see the maiden. And Arthur, and all his companions, and his whole Court, were glad concerning the maiden. And certain were they all, that had her array been suitable to her beauty, they had never seen a maid fairer than she. And Arthur gave away the maiden to Geraint. And the usual bond made between two persons was made between Geraint and the maiden, and the choicest of all Gwenhwyvar's apparel was given to the maiden; and thus arrayed, she appeared comely and graceful to all who beheld her. And that day and that night were spent in abundance of minstrelsy, and ample gifts of liquor, and a multitude of games. And when it was time for them to go to sleep, they went. And in the chamber where the couch of Arthur and Gwenhwyvar was, the couch of Geraint and Enid was prepared. And from that time she became his bride. And the next day Arthur satisfied all the claimants upon Geraint with bountiful gifts. And the maiden took up her abode in the palace, and she had many companions, both men and women, and there was no maiden more esteemed than she in the Island of Britain.

Then spake Gwenhwyvar. "Rightly did I judge," said she, "concerning the head of the stag, that it should not be given to any until Geraint's return; and, behold, here is a fit occasion for bestowing it. Let it be given to Enid, the daughter of Ynywl, the most illustrious maiden. And I do not believe that any will begrudge it her, for between her and every one here there exists nothing but love and friendship." Much applauded was this by them all, and by Arthur also. And the head of the stag was given to Enid. And thereupon her fame increased, and her friends thenceforward became more in number than before. And Geraint from that time forth loved the stag, and the tournament, and hard encounters; and he came victorious from them all. And a year, and a second, and a third, he proceeded thus, until his fame had flown over the face of the kingdom.

And once upon a time, Arthur was holding his Court at Caerlleon upon Usk, at Whitsuntide. And, behold, there came to him ambassadors, wise and prudent, full of knowledge, and eloquent of speech, and they saluted Arthur. "Heaven prosper you," said Arthur, "and the welcome of Heaven be unto you. And whence do you come?" "We come, Lord," said they, "from Cornwall; and we are ambassadors from Erbin the son of Custennin, thy uncle, and our mission is unto thee. And he greets thee well, as an uncle should greet his nephew, and as a vassal should greet his lord. And he represents unto thee that he waxes heavy and feeble, and is advancing in years. And the neighbouring chiefs knowing this, grow insolent towards him, and covet his land and possessions. And he earnestly beseeches thee, Lord, to permit Geraint his son to return to him, to protect his possessions, and to become acquainted with his boundaries. And unto him he represents that it were better for him to spend the flower of his youth, and the prime of his age, in preserving his own boundaries, than in tournaments, which are productive of no profit, although he obtains glory in them."

"Well," said Arthur, "go, and divest yourselves of your accoutrements, and take food, and refresh yourselves after your fatigues; and before you go forth hence you shall have an answer." And they went to eat. And Arthur considered that it would go hard with him to let Geraint depart from him and from his Court; neither did he think it fair that his cousin should be restrained from going to protect his dominions and his boundaries, seeing that his father was unable to do so. No less was the grief and regret of Gwenhwyvar, and all her women, and all her damsels, through fear that the maiden would leave them. And that day and that night were spent in abundance of feasting. And Arthur showed Geraint the cause of the mission, and of the coming of the ambassadors to him out of Cornwall. "Truly," said Geraint, "be it to my advantage or disadvantage, Lord, I will do according to thy will concerning this embassy." "Behold," said Arthur, "though it grieves me to part with thee, it is my counsel that thou go to dwell in thine own dominions, and to defend thy boundaries, and to take with thee to accompany thee as many as thou wilt of those thou lovest best among my faithful ones, and among thy friends, and among thy companions in arms." "Heaven reward thee; and this will I do," said Geraint. "What discourse," said Gwenhwyvar, "do I hear between you? Is it of those who are to conduct Geraint to his country?" "It is," said Arthur. "Then is it needful for me to consider," said she, "concerning companions and a provision for the lady that is with me?" "Thou wilt do well," said Arthur.

And that night they went to sleep. And the next day the ambassadors were permitted to depart, and they were told that Geraint should follow them. And on the third day Geraint set forth, and many went with him. Gwalchmai the son of Gwyar, and Riogonedd the son of the king of Ireland, and Ondyaw the son of the duke of Burgandy, Gwilim the son of the ruler of the Franks, Howel the son of Emyr of Brittany, Elivry, and Nawkyrd, Gwynn the son of Tringad, Goreu the son of Custennin, Gweir Gwrhyd Vawr, Garannaw the son of Golithmer, Peredur the son of Evrawc, Gwynnllogell, Gwyr a judge in the Court of Arthur, Dyvyr the son of Alun of Dyved, Gwrei Gwalstawd Ieithoedd, Bedwyr the son of Bedrawd, Hadwry the son of Gwryon, Kai the son of Kynyr, Odyar the Frank, the Steward of Arthur's Court, and Edeyrn the son of Nudd. Said Geraint, "I think that I shall have enough of knighthood with me." "Yes," said Arthur, "but it will not be fitting for thee to take Edeyrn with thee, although he is well, until peace shall be made between him and Gwenhwyvar." "Gwenhwyvar can permit him to go with me, if he gives sureties." "If she please, she can let him go without sureties, for enough of pain and affliction has he suffered for the insult which the maiden received from the dwarf." "Truly," said Gwenhwyvar, "since it seems well to thee and to Geraint, I will do this gladly, Lord." Then she permitted Edeyrn freely to depart. And many there were who accompanied Geraint, and they set forth; and never was there seen a fairer host journeying towards the Severn. And on the other side of the Severn were the nobles of Erbin the son of Custennin, and his foster father at their head, to welcome Geraint with gladness; and many of the women of the Court, with his mother, came to receive Enid the daughter of Ynywl, his wife. And there was great rejoicing and gladness throughout the whole Court, and throughout all the country, concerning Geraint, because of the greatness of their love towards him, and of the greatness of the fame which he had gained since he went from amongst them, and because he was come to take possession of his dominions, and to preserve his boundaries. And they came to the Court. And in the Court they had ample entertainment, and a multitude of gifts, and abundance of liquor, and a sufficiency of service, and a variety of minstrelsy and of games. And to do honour to Geraint, all the chief men of the country were invited that night to visit him. And they passed that day and that night in the utmost enjoyment. And at dawn next day Erbin arose, and summoned to him Geraint, and the noble persons who had borne him company. And he said to Geraint, "I am a feeble and an aged man, and whilst I was able to maintain the dominion for thee and for myself, I did so. But thou art young, and in the flower of thy vigour and of thy youth: henceforth do thou preserve thy possessions." "Truly," said Geraint, "with my consent thou shalt not give the power over thy dominions at this time into my hands, and thou shall not take me from Arthur's Court." "Into thy hands will I give them," said Erbin, "and this day also shalt thou receive the homage of thy subjects."

Then said Gwalchmai, "It were better for thee to satisfy those who have boons to ask, to-day, and to-morrow thou canst receive the homage of thy dominions." So all that had boons to ask were summoned into one place. And Kadyrieith came to them, to know what were their requests. And every one asked that which he desired. And the followers of Arthur began to make gifts and immediately the men of Cornwall came, and gave also. And they were not long in giving, so eager was every one to bestow gifts. And of those who came to ask gifts, none departed unsatisfied. And that day and that night were spent in the utmost enjoyment.

And the next day, at dawn, Erbin desired Geraint to send messengers to the men, to ask them whether it was displeasing to them that he should come to receive their homage, and whether they had anything to object to him. Then Geraint sent ambassadors to the men of Cornwall, to ask them this. And they all said that it would be the fulness of joy and honour to them for Geraint to come and receive their homage. So he received the homage of such as were there. And they remained with him till the third night. And the day after the followers of Arthur intended to go away. "It is too soon for you to go away yet," said he, "stay with me until I have finished receiving the homage of my chief men, who have agreed to come to me." And they remained with him until he had done so. Then they set forth towards the Court of Arthur; and Geraint went to bear them company, and Enid also, as far as Diganhwy: there they parted. Then Ondyaw the son of the duke of Burgundy said to Geraint, "Go first of all, and visit the uttermost parts of thy dominions, and see well to the boundaries of thy territories; and if thou hast any trouble respecting them, send unto thy companions." "Heaven reward thee," said Geraint, "and this will I do." And Geraint journeyed to the uttermost part of his dominions. And experienced guides, and the chief men of his country, went with him. And the furthermost point that they showed him he kept possession of.

And, as he had been used to do when he was at Arthur's Court, he frequented tournaments. And he became acquainted with valiant and mighty men, until he had gained as much fame there as he had formerly done elsewhere. And he enriched his Court, and his companions, and his nobles, with the best horses, and the best arms, and with the best and most valuable jewels, and he ceased not until his fame had flown over the face of the whole kingdom. And when he knew that it was thus, he began to love ease and pleasure, for there was no one who was worth his opposing. And he loved his wife, and liked to continue in the palace, with minstrelsy and diversions. And for a long time he abode at home. And after that he began to shut himself up in the chamber of his wife, and he took no delight in anything besides, insomuch that he gave up the friendship of his nobles, together with his hunting and his amusements, and lost the hearts of all the host in his Court; and there was murmuring and scoffing concerning him among the inhabitants of the palace, on account of his relinquishing so completely their companionship for the love of his wife. And these tidings came to Erbin. And when Erbin had heard these things, he spoke unto Enid, and enquired of her whether it was she that had caused Geraint to act thus, and to forsake his people and his hosts. "Not I, by my confession unto Heaven," said she; "there is nothing more hateful to me than this." And she knew not what she should do, for, although it was hard for her to own this to Geraint, yet was it not more easy for her to listen to what she heard without warning Geraint concerning it. And she was very sorrowful.

And one morning in the summer time, they were upon their couch, and Geraint lay upon the edge of it. And Enid was without sleep in the apartment, which had windows of glass. And the sun shone upon the couch. And the clothes had slipped from off his arms and his breast, and he was asleep. Then she gazed upon the marvellous beauty of his appearance, and she said, "Alas, and am I the cause that these arms and this breast have lost their glory and the warlike fame which they once so richly enjoyed!" And as she said this, the tears dropped from her eyes, and they fell upon his breast. And the tears she shed, and the words she had spoken, awoke him; and another thing contributed to awaken him, and that was the idea that it was not in thinking of him that she spoke thus, but that it was because she loved some other man more than him, and that she wished for other society, and thereupon Geraint was troubled in his mind, and he called his squire;

and when he came to him, "Go quickly," said he, "and prepare my horse and my arms, and make them ready. And do thou arise," said he to Enid, "and apparel thyself; and cause thy horse to be accoutred, and clothe thee in the worst riding dress that thou hast in thy possession. And evil betide me," said he, "if thou returnest here until thou knowest whether I have lost my strength so completely as thou didst say. And if it be so, it will then be easy for thee to seek the society thou didst wish for of him of whom thou wast thinking." So she arose, and clothed herself in her meanest garments. "I know nothing, Lord," said she, "of thy meaning." "Neither wilt thou know at this time," said he.

Then Geraint went to see Erbin. "Sir," said he, "I am going upon a quest, and I am not certain when I may come back. Take heed, therefore, unto thy possessions, until my return." "I will do so," said he, "but it is strange to me that thou shouldst go so suddenly. And who will proceed with thee, since thou art not strong enough to traverse the land of Lloegyr alone." "But one person only will go with me." "Heaven counsel thee, my son," said Erbin, "and may many attach themselves to thee in Lloegyr." Then went Geraint to the place where his horse was, and it was equipped with foreign armour, heavy and shining. And he desired Enid to mount her horse, and to ride forward, and to keep a long way before him. "And whatever thou mayest see, and whatever thou mayest hear, concerning me," said he, "do thou not turn back. And unless I speak unto thee, say not thou one word either." And they set forward. And he did not choose the pleasantest and most frequented road, but that which was the wildest and most beset by thieves, and robbers, and venomous animals. And they came to a high road, which they followed till they saw a vast forest, and they went towards it, and they saw four armed horsemen come forth from the forest. When they had beheld them, one of them said to the other, "Behold, here is a good occasion for us to capture two horses and armour, and a lady likewise; for this we shall have no difficulty in doing against yonder single knight, who hangs his head so pensively and heavily." And Enid heard this discourse, and she knew not what she should do through fear of Geraint, who had told her to be silent. "The vengeance of Heaven be upon me," she said, "if I would not rather receive my death from his hand than from the hand of any other; and though he should slay me, yet will I speak to him, lest I should have the misery to witness his death." [36a] So she waited for Geraint until he came near to her. "Lord," said she, "didst thou hear the words of those men concerning thee?" Then he lifted up his eyes, and looked at her angrily. "Thou hadst only," said he, "to hold thy peace as I bade thee. I wish but for silence and not for warning. [36b] And though thou shouldst desire to see my defeat and my death by the hands of those men, yet do I feel no dread." Then the foremost of them couched his lance, and rushed upon Geraint. And he received him, and that not feebly. But he let the thrust go by him, while he struck the horseman upon the centre of his shield in such a manner, that his shield was split, and his armour broken, and so that a cubit's length of the shaft of Geraint's lance passed through his body, and sent him to the earth the length of the lance over his horse's crupper. Then the second horseman attacked him furiously, being wroth at the death of his companion. But with one thrust Geraint overthrew him also, and killed him as he had done the other. Then the third set upon him, and he killed him in like manner. And thus also he slew the fourth. Sad and sorrowful was the maiden as she saw all this. Geraint dismounted his horse, and took the arms of the men he had slain, and placed them upon their saddles, and tied together the reins of their horses, and he mounted his horse again. "Behold what thou must do," said he, "take the four horses, and drive them before thee, and proceed forward, as I bade thee just now. And say not one word unto me, unless I speak first unto thee. And I declare unto Heaven," said he, "if thou doest not thus, it will be to thy cost." "I will do, as far as I can, Lord," said she, "according to thy desire." Then they went forward through the forest; and when they left the forest, they came to a vast plain, in the centre of which was a group of thickly tangled copse-wood; and from out thereof they beheld three horsemen coming towards them, well equipped with armour, both they and their horses. Then the maiden looked steadfastly upon them; and when they had come near, she heard them say one to another, "Behold, here is a good arrival for us, here are coming for us four horses and four suits of armour. We shall easily obtain them spite of yonder dolorous knight, and the maiden also will fall into our power." "This is but too true," said she to herself, "for my husband is tired with his former combat. The vengeance of Heaven will be upon me, unless I warn him of this." So the maiden waited until Geraint came up to her. "Lord," said she, "dost thou not hear the discourse of yonder men concerning thee?" "What was it?" asked he. "They say to one another, that they will easily obtain all this spoil." "I declare to Heaven," he answered, "that their words are less grievous to me than that thou wilt not be silent, and abide by my counsel." "My Lord," said she, "I feared lest they should surprise thee unawares." "Hold thy peace then," said he, "do not I desire silence?" [38] And thereupon one of the horsemen couched his lance, and attacked Geraint. And he made a thrust at him, which he thought would be very effective; but Geraint received it carelessly, and struck it aside, and then he rushed upon him, and aimed at the centre of his person, and from the shock of man and horse, the quantity of his armour did not avail him, and the head of the lance and part of the shaft passed through him, so that he was carried to the ground an arm and a spear's length over the crupper of his horse. And both the other horsemen came forward in their turn, but their onset was not more successful than that of their companion. And the maiden stood by, looking at all this; and on the one hand she was in trouble lest Geraint should be wounded in his encounter with the men, and on the other hand she was joyful to see him victorious. Then Geraint dismounted, and bound the three suits of armour upon the three saddles, and he fastened the reins of all the horses together, so that he had seven horses with him. And he mounted his own horse, and commanded the maiden to drive forward the others. "It is no more use for me to speak to thee than to refrain, for thou wilt not attend to my advice." "I will do so, as far I am able, Lord," said she; "but I cannot conceal from thee the fierce and threatening words which I may hear against thee, Lord, from such strange people as those that haunt this wilderness." "I declare to Heaven," said he, "that I desire nought but silence; therefore, hold thy peace." [39] "I will, Lord, while I can." And the maiden went on with the horses before her, and she pursued her way straight onwards. And from the copse-wood already mentioned, they journeyed over a vast and dreary open plain. And at a great distance from them they beheld a wood, and they could see neither end nor boundary to the wood, except on that side that was nearest to them, and they went towards it. Then there came from out the wood five horsemen, eager, and bold, and mighty, and strong, mounted upon chargers that were powerful, and large of bone, and high-mettled, and proudly snorting, and both the men and the horses were well equipped with arms. And when they drew near to them, Enid heard them say, "Behold, here is a fine booty coming to us, which we shall obtain easily and without labour, for we shall have no trouble in taking all those horses and arms, and the lady also, from yonder single knight, so doleful and sad."

Sorely grieved was the maiden upon hearing this discourse, so that she knew not in the world what she should do. At last, however, she determined to warn Geraint; so she turned her horse's head towards him. "Lord," said she, "if thou hadst heard as I did what yonder horsemen said concerning thee, thy heaviness would be greater than it is." Angrily and bitterly did Geraint smile upon her, and he said, "Thee do I hear doing everything that I forbade thee; but it may be that thou wilt repent this yet." And immediately, behold, the men met them, and victoriously and gallantly did Geraint overcome them all five. And he placed the five suits of armour upon the five saddles, and tied together the reins of the twelve horses, and gave them in charge to Enid. "I know not," said he, "what good it is for me to order thee; but this time I charge thee in an especial manner." So the maiden went forward towards the wood, keeping in advance of Geraint, as he had desired her; and it grieved him as much as his wrath would permit, to see a maiden so illustrious as she having so much trouble with the care of the horses. Then they reached the wood, and it was both deep and vast; and in the wood night overtook them. "Ah, maiden," said he, "it is vain to attempt proceeding forward!" "Well, Lord," said she, "whatsoever thou wishest, we will do." "It will be best for us," he answered, "to turn out of the wood, and to rest, and wait for the day, in order to pursue our journey." "That will we, gladly," said she. And they did so. Having dismounted himself, he took her down from her horse. "I cannot, by any means, refrain from sleep, through weariness," said he. "Do thou, therefore, watch the horses, and sleep not." "I will, Lord," said she. Then he went to sleep in his armour, and thus passed the night, which was not long at that season. And when she saw the dawn of day appear, she looked around her, to see if he were waking, and thereupon he woke. "My Lord," she said, "I have desired to awake thee for some time." But he spake nothing to her about fatigue, [40] as he had desired her to be silent. Then he arose, and said unto her, "Take the horses, and ride on; and keep straight on before thee as thou didst yesterday." And early in the day they left the wood, and they came to an open country, with meadows on one hand, and mowers mowing the meadows. And there was a river before them, and the horses bent down, and drank the water. And they went up out of the river by a lofty steep; and there they met a slender stripling, with a satchel about his neck, and they saw that there was something in the satchel, but they knew not what it was. And he had a small blue pitcher in his hand, and a bowl on the mouth of the pitcher. And the youth saluted Geraint. "Heaven prosper thee," said Geraint, "and whence dost thou come?" "I come," said he, "from the city that lies before thee. My Lord," he added, "will it be displeasing to thee, if I ask whence thou comest also?" "By no means—through yonder wood did I come." "Thou camest not through the wood to-day." "No," he replied, "we were in the wood last night." "I warrant," said the youth, "that thy condition there last night was not the most pleasant, and that thou hadst neither meat nor drink." "No, by my faith," said he. "Wilt thou follow my counsel," said the youth, "and take thy meal from me?" "What sort of meal?" he enquired. "The breakfast which is sent for yonder mowers, nothing less than bread and meat, and wine; and if thou wilt, Sir, they shall have none of it." "I will," said he, "and Heaven reward thee for it."

So Geraint alighted, and the youth took the maiden from off her horse. Then they washed, and took their repast. And the youth cut the bread in slices, and gave them drink, and served them withal. And when they had finished, the youth arose, and said to Geraint, "My Lord, with thy permission I will now go and fetch some food for the mowers." "Go, first, to the town," said Geraint, "and take a lodging for me in the best place that thou knowest, and the most commodious one for the horses, and take thou whichever horse and arms thou choosest in payment for thy service and thy gift." "Heaven reward thee, Lord," said the youth, "and this would be ample to repay services much greater than those I rendered unto thee." And to the town went the youth, and he took the best and the most pleasant lodgings that he knew; and after that he went to the palace, having the horse and armour with him, and proceeded to the place where the Earl was, and told him all his adventure. "I go now, Lord," said he, "to meet the young man, and to conduct him to his lodging." "Go gladly," said the Earl, "and right joyfully shall he be received here, if he so come." And the youth went to meet Geraint, and told him that he would be received gladly by the Earl in his own palace; but he would go only to his lodgings. And he had a goodly chamber, in which was plenty of straw, and draperies, and a spacious and commodious place he had for the horses, and the youth prepared for them plenty of provender. And after they had disarrayed themselves, Geraint spoke thus to Enid: "Go," said he, "to the other side of the chamber, and come not to this side of the house; and thou mayest call to thee the woman of the house, if thou wilt." "I will do, Lord," said she, "as thou sayest." And thereupon the man of the house came to Geraint, and welcomed him. "Oh, chieftain," he said, "hast thou taken thy meal?" "I have," said he. Then the youth spoke to him, and enquired if he would not drink something before he met the Earl. "Truly, I will," said he. So the youth went into the town, and brought them drink. And they drank. "I must needs sleep," said Geraint. "Well," said the youth, "and whilst thou sleepest, I will go to see the Earl." "Go, gladly," he said, "and come here again when I require thee." And Geraint went to sleep, and so did Enid also.

And the youth came to the place where the Earl was, and the Earl asked him where the lodgings of the knight were, and he told him. "I must go," said the youth, "to wait on him in the evening." "Go," answered the Earl, "and greet him well from me, and tell him that in the evening I will go to see him." "This will I do," said the youth. So he came when it was time for them to awake. And they arose, and went forth. And when it was time for them to take their food they took it. And the youth served them. And Geraint enquired of the man of the house, whether there were any of his companions that he wished to invite to him, and he said that there were. "Bring them hither, and entertain them at my cost with the best thou canst buy in the town."

And the man of the house brought there those whom he chose, and feasted them at Geraint's expense. Thereupon, behold, the Earl came to visit Geraint, and his twelve honourable knights with him. And Geraint rose up, and welcomed him. "Heaven preserve thee," said the Earl. Then they all sat down according to their precedence in honour. And the Earl conversed with Geraint and enquired of him the object of his journey. "I have none," he replied, "but to seek adventures, and to follow my own inclination." Then the Earl cast his eye upon Enid, and he looked at her steadfastly. And he thought he had never seen a maiden fairer or more comely than she. And he set all his thoughts and his affections upon her. Then he asked of Geraint, "Have I thy permission to go and converse with yonder maiden, for I see that she is apart from thee?" "Thou hast it, gladly," said he. So the Earl went to the place where the maiden was, and spake with her. "Ah, maiden," said he, "it cannot be pleasant to thee to journey thus with yonder man!" "It is not unpleasant to me," said she, "to journey the same road that he journeys." "Thou hast neither youths nor maidens to serve thee," said he. "Truly," she replied, "it is more pleasant for me to follow yonder man than to be served by youths and maidens." "I will give thee good counsel," said he. "All my Earldom will I place in thy possession, if thou wilt dwell with me." "That will I not, by Heaven," she said, "yonder man was the first to whom my faith was ever pledged; and shall I prove inconstant to him?" "Thou art in the wrong," said the Earl; "if I slay the man yonder, I can keep thee with me as long as I choose; and when thou no longer pleasest me, I can turn thee away. But if thou goest with me by thy own good will, I protest that our union shall continue eternal and undivided as long as I remain alive." Then she pondered these words of his, and she considered that it was advisable to encourage him in his request. "Behold, then, chieftain, this is most expedient for thee to do to save me any needless imputation; come here to-morrow, and take me away as though I knew nothing thereof." "I will do so," said he. So he arose, and took his leave, and went forth with his attendants. And she told not then to Geraint any of the conversation which she had had with the Earl, lest it should rouse his anger, and cause him uneasiness and care.

And at the usual hour they went to sleep. And at the beginning of the night Enid slept a little; and at midnight she arose, and placed all Geraint's armour together, so that it might be ready to put on. And although fearful of her errand, she came to the side of Geraint's bed; and she spoke to him softly and gently, saying, "My Lord, arise, and clothe thyself, for these were the words of the Earl to me, and his intention concerning me." So she told Geraint all that had passed. And although he was wroth with her, he took warning, and clothed himself. And she lighted a candle, that he might have light to do so. "Leave there the candle," said he, "and desire the man of the house to come here." Then she went, and the man of the house came to him. "Dost thou know how much I owe thee?" asked Geraint. "I think thou owest but little." "Take the eleven horses and the eleven suits of armour." "Heaven reward thee, Lord," said he, "but I spent not the value of one suit of armour upon thee." "For that reason," said he, "thou wilt be the richer. And now wilt thou come to guide me out of the town?" "I will, gladly," said he, "and in which direction dost thou intend to go?" "I wish to leave the town by a different way from that by which I entered it." So the man of the lodgings accompanied him as far as he desired. Then he bade the maiden to go on before him; and she did so, and went straight forward, and his host returned home. And he had only just reached his house, when, behold, the greatest tumult approached that was ever heard. And when he looked out he saw fourscore knights in complete armour around the house, with the Earl Dwrm at their head. "Where is the knight that was here?" said the Earl. "By thy hand," said he, "he went hence some time ago." "Wherefore, villain," said he, "didst thou let him go without informing me?" "My Lord, thou didst not command me to do so, else would I not have allowed him to depart." "What way dost thou think that he took?" "I know not, except that he went along the high road." And they turned their horses' heads that way, and seeing the tracks of the horses upon the high road, they followed. And when the maiden beheld the dawning of the day, she looked behind her, and saw vast clouds of dust coming nearer and nearer to her. And thereupon she became uneasy, and she thought that it was the Earl and his host coming after them. And thereupon she beheld a knight appearing through the mist. "By my faith," said she, "though he should slay me, it were better for me to receive my death at his hands, than to see him killed without warning him." "My Lord," she said to him, "seest thou yonder man hastening after thee, and many others with him?" "I do see him," said he, "and in despite of all my orders, I see that thou wilt never keep silence." Then he turned upon the knight, and with the first thrust he threw him down under his horse's feet. And as long as there remained one of the fourscore knights, he overthrew every one of them at the first onset. And from the weakest to the strongest, they all attacked him one after the other, except the Earl: and last of all the Earl came against him also. And he broke his lance, and then he broke a second. But Geraint turned upon him, and struck him with his lance upon the centre of his shield, so that by that single thrust the shield was split, and all his armour broken, and he himself was brought over his horse's crupper to the ground, and was in peril of his life. And Geraint drew near to him; and at the noise of the trampling of his horse the Earl revived. "Mercy, Lord," said he to Geraint. And Geraint granted him mercy. But through the hardness of the ground where they had fallen, and the violence of the stroke which they had received, there was not a single knight amongst them that escaped without receiving a fall, mortally severe, and grievously painful, and desperately wounding, from the hand of Geraint.

And Geraint journeyed along the high road that was before him, and the maiden went on first; and near them they beheld a valley which was the fairest ever seen, and which had a large river running through it; and there was a bridge over the river, and the high road led to the bridge. And above the bridge, upon the opposite side of the river, they beheld a fortified town, the fairest ever seen. And as they approached the bridge, Geraint saw coming towards him from a thick copse a man mounted upon a large and lofty steed, even of pace and spirited though tractable. "Ah, knight," said Geraint, "whence comest thou?" "I come," said he "from the valley below us." "Canst thou tell me," said Geraint, "who is the owner of this fair valley and yonder walled town?" "I will tell thee, willingly," said he, "Gwiffert Petit he is called by the Franks, but the Welsh call him the Little King." "Can I go by yonder bridge," said Geraint, "and by the lower highway that is beneath the town?" Said the knight, "Thou canst not go by his tower [47a] on the other side of the bridge, unless thou dost intend to combat him; because it is his custom to encounter every knight that comes upon his lands." "I declare to Heaven," said Geraint, "that I will, nevertheless, pursue my journey that way." [47b] "If thou dost so," said the knight, "thou wilt probably meet with shame and disgrace in reward for thy daring." [48a] Then Geraint proceeded along the road that led to the town, and the road brought him to a ground that was hard, and rugged, and high, and ridgy. [48b] And as he journeyed thus, he beheld a knight following him upon a war-horse, strong, and large, and proudly-stepping, and wide-hoofed, and broad-chested. And he never saw a man of smaller stature than he who was upon the horse. And both he and his horse were completely armed. When he had overtaken Geraint he said to him, "Tell me, chieftain, whether it is through ignorance or through presumption that thou seekest to insult my dignity, and to infringe my rules?" "Nay," answered Geraint, "I knew not that this road was forbid to any." "Thou didst know it," said the other; "come with me to my Court, to do me satisfaction." "That will I not, by my faith," said Geraint; "I would not go even to thy Lord's Court, excepting Arthur were thy Lord." "By the hand of Arthur himself," said the knight, "I will have satisfaction of thee, or receive my overthrow at thy hands." And immediately they charged one another. And a squire of his came to serve him with lances as he broke them. And they gave each other such hard and severe strokes, that their shields lost all their colour. But it was very difficult for Geraint to fight with him on account of his small size, for he was hardly able to get a full aim at him with all the efforts he could make. [49] And they fought thus until their horses were brought down upon their knees; and at length Geraint threw the knight headlong to the ground; and then they fought on foot, and they gave one another blows so boldly fierce, so frequent, and so severely powerful, that their helmets were pierced, and their skullcaps were broken, and their arms were shattered, and the light of their eyes was darkened by sweat and blood. At the last Geraint became enraged, and he called to him all his strength; and boldly angry, and swiftly resolute, and furiously determined, he lifted up his sword, and struck him on the crown of his head a blow so mortally painful, so violent, so fierce, and so penetrating, that it cut through all his head armour, and his skin, and his flesh, until it wounded the very bone, and the sword flew out of the hand of the Little King to the furthest end of the plain, and he besought Geraint that he would have mercy and compassion upon him. "Though thou hast been neither courteous nor just," said Geraint, "thou shalt have mercy, upon condition that thou wilt become my ally, and engage never to fight against me again, but to come to my assistance whenever thou hearest of my being in trouble." "This will I do, gladly, Lord," said he. So he pledged him his faith thereof. "And now, Lord, come with me," said he, "to my Court yonder, to recover from thy weariness and fatigue." "That will I not, by Heaven," said he.

Then Gwiffert Petit beheld Enid where she stood, and it grieved him to see one of her noble mien appear so deeply afflicted. And he said to Geraint, "My Lord, thou doest wrong not to take repose, and refresh thyself awhile; for, if thou meetest with any difficulty in thy present condition, it will not be easy for thee to surmount it." But Geraint would do no other than proceed on his journey, and he mounted his horse in pain, and all covered with blood. And the maiden went on first, and they proceeded towards the wood which they saw before them.

And the heat of the sun was very great, and through the blood and sweat, Geraint's armour cleaved to his flesh; and when they came into the wood, he stood under a tree, to avoid the sun's heat; and his wounds pained him more than they had done at the time when he received them. And the maiden stood under another tree. And, lo! they heard the sound of horns, and a tumultuous noise, and the occasion of it was, that Arthur and his company had come down to the wood. And while Geraint was considering which way he should go to avoid them, behold, he was espied by a foot page, who was an attendant on the Steward of the Household, and he went to the steward, and told him what kind of man he had seen in the wood. Then the steward caused his horse to be saddled, and he took his lance and his shield, and went to the place where Geraint was. "Ah, knight!" said he, "what dost thou here?" "I am standing under a shady tree, to avoid the heat and the rays of the sun." "Wherefore is thy journey, and who art thou?" "I seek adventures, and go where I list." "Indeed," said Kai, "then come with me to see Arthur, who is here hard by." "That will I not, by Heaven," said Geraint. "Thou must needs come," said Kai. Then Geraint knew who he was, but Kai did not know Geraint. And Kai attacked Geraint as best as he could. And Geraint became wroth, and he struck him with the shaft of his lance, so that he rolled headlong to the ground. But chastisement worse than this would he not inflict on him.

Scared and wildly Kai arose, and he mounted his horse, and went back to his lodging. And thence he proceeded to Gwalchmai's tent. "Oh, Sir," said he to Gwalchmai, "I was told by one of the attendants, that he saw in the wood above a wounded knight, having on battered armour, and if thou dost right, thou wilt go and see if this be true." "I care not if I do so," said Gwalchmai. "Take, then, thy horse, and some of thy armour," said Kai, "for I hear that he is not over-courteous to those who approach him." So Gwalchmai took his spear and his shield, and mounted his horse, and came to the spot where Geraint was. "Sir Knight," said he, "wherefore is thy journey?" "I journey for my own pleasure, and to seek the adventures of the world." "Wilt thou tell me who thou art, or wilt thou come and visit Arthur, who is near at hand?" "I will make no alliance with thee, nor will I go and visit Arthur," said he. And he knew that it was Gwalchmai, but Gwalchmai knew him not. "I purpose not to leave thee," said Gwalchmai, "till I know who thou art." And he charged him with his lance, and struck him on his shield, so that the shaft was shivered into splinters, and their horses were front to front. Then Gwalchmai gazed fixedly upon him, and he knew him. "Ah, Geraint," said he, "is it thou that art here?" "I am not Geraint," said he. "Geraint thou art, by Heaven," he replied, "and a wretched and insane expedition is this." Then he looked around, and beheld Enid, and he welcomed her gladly. "Geraint," said Gwalchmai, "come thou, and see Arthur; he is thy lord and thy cousin." "I will not," said he, "for I am not in a fit state to go and see any one." Thereupon, behold, one of the pages came after Gwalchmai, to speak to him. So he sent him to apprise Arthur that Geraint was there wounded, and that he would not go to visit him, and that it was pitiable to see the plight that he was in. And this he did without Geraint's knowledge, inasmuch as he spoke in a whisper to the page. "Entreat Arthur," said he, "to have his tent brought near to the road, for he will not meet him willingly, and it is not easy to compel him in the mood he is in." So the page came to Arthur, and told him this. And he caused his tent to be removed unto the side of the road. And the maiden rejoiced in her heart. And Gwalchmai led Geraint onwards along the road, till they came to the place where Arthur was encamped, and the pages were pitching his tent by the road-side. "Lord," said Geraint, "all hail unto thee." "Heaven prosper thee; and who art thou?" said Arthur. "It is Geraint," said Gwalchmai, "and of his own free will would he not come to meet thee." "Verily," said Arthur, "he is bereft of his reason." Then came Enid, and saluted Arthur. "Heaven protect thee," said he. And thereupon he caused one of the pages to take her from her horse. "Alas! Enid," said Arthur, "what expedition is this?" "I know not, Lord," said she, "save that it behoves me to journey by the same road that he journeys." "My Lord," said Geraint, "with thy permission we will depart." "Whither wilt thou go?" said Arthur. "Thou canst not proceed now, unless it be unto thy death." [53] "He will not suffer himself to be invited by me," said Gwalchmai. "But by me he will," said Arthur; "and, moreover, he does not go from here until he is healed." "I had rather, Lord," said Geraint, "that thou wouldest let me go forth." "That will I not, I declare to Heaven," said he. Then he caused a maiden to be sent for to conduct Enid to the tent where Gwenhwyvar's chamber was. And Gwenhwyvar and all her women were joyful at her coming, and they took off her riding dress, and placed other garments upon her. Arthur also called Kadyrieith, and ordered him to pitch a tent for Geraint, and the physicians, and he enjoined him to provide him with abundance of all that might be requisite for him. And Kadyrieith did as he had commanded him. And Morgan Tud and his disciples were brought to Geraint.

And Arthur and his hosts remained there nearly a month, whilst Geraint was being healed. And when he was fully recovered, Geraint came to Arthur, and asked his permission to depart. "I know not if thou art quite well." "In truth I am, Lord," said Geraint. "I shall not believe thee concerning that, but the physicians that were with thee." So Arthur caused the physicians to be summoned to him, and asked them if it were true. "It is true, Lord," said Morgan Tud. So the next day Arthur permitted him to go forth, and he pursued his journey. And on the same day Arthur removed thence. And Geraint desired Enid to go on, and to keep before him, as she had formerly done. And she went forward along the high road. And as they journeyed thus, they heard an exceeding loud wailing near to them. "Stay thou here," said he, "and I will go and see what is the cause of this wailing." "I will," said she. Then he went forward into an open glade that was near the road. And in the glade he saw two horses, one having a man's saddle, and the other a woman's saddle upon it. And, behold, there was a knight lying dead in his armour, and a young damsel in a riding dress standing over him, lamenting. "Ah! Lady," said Geraint, "what hath befallen thee?" "Behold," she answered, "I journeyed here with my beloved husband, when, lo! three giants came upon us, and without any cause in the world, they slew him." "Which way went they hence?" said Geraint. "Yonder by the high road," she replied. So he returned to Enid. "Go," said he, "to the lady that is below yonder, and await me there till I come." She was sad when he ordered her to do thus, but nevertheless she went to the damsel, whom it was ruth to hear, and she felt certain that Geraint would never return. Meanwhile Geraint followed the giants, and overtook them. And each of them was greater of stature than three other men, and a huge club was on the shoulder of each. Then he rushed upon one of them, and thrust his lance through his body. And having drawn it forth again, he pierced another of them through likewise. But the third turned upon him, and struck him with his club, so that he split his shield, and crushed his shoulder, and opened his wounds anew, and all his blood began to flow from him. But Geraint drew his sword, and attacked the giant, and gave him a blow on the crown of his head so severe, and fierce, and violent, that his head and his neck were split down to his shoulders, and he fell dead. So Geraint left him thus, and returned to Enid. And when he saw her, he fell down lifeless from his horse. Piercing, and loud, and thrilling was the cry that Enid uttered. And she came and stood over him where he had fallen. And at the sound of her cries came the Earl of Limours, and the host that journeyed with him, whom her lamentations brought out of their road. And the Earl said to Enid, "Alas, Lady, what hath befallen thee?" "Ah! good Sir," said she, "the only man I have loved, or ever shall love, is slain." Then he said to the other, "And what is the cause of thy grief?" "They have slain my beloved husband also," said she. "And who was it that slew them?" "Some giants," she answered, "slew my best beloved, and the other knight went in pursuit of them, and came back in the state thou seest, his blood flowing excessively; but it appears to me that he did not leave the giants without killing some of them, if not all." The Earl caused the knight that was dead to be buried, but he thought that there still remained some life in Geraint; and to see if he yet would live, he had him carried with him in the hollow of his shield, and upon a bier. And the two damsels went to the court; and when they arrived there, Geraint was placed upon a litter-couch in front of the table that was in the hall. Then they all took off their travelling gear, and the Earl besought Enid to do the same, and to clothe herself in other garments. "I will not, by Heaven," said she. "Ah! Lady," said he, "be not so sorrowful for this matter." "It were hard to persuade me to be otherwise," said she. "I will act towards thee in such wise, that thou needest not be sorrowful, whether yonder knight live or die. Behold, a good Earldom, together with myself, will I bestow on thee; be, therefore, happy and joyful." "I declare to Heaven," said she, "that henceforth I shall never be joyful while I live." "Come, then," said he, "and eat." "No, by Heaven, I will not," she answered. "But by Heaven thou shalt," said he. So he took her with him to the table against her will, and many times desired her to eat. "I call Heaven to witness," said she, "that I will not eat until the man that is upon yonder bier shall eat likewise." "Thou canst not fulfil that," said the Earl, "yonder man is dead already." "I will prove that I can," said she. Then he offered her a goblet of liquor. "Drink this goblet," he said, "and it will cause thee to change thy mind." "Evil betide me," she answered, "if I drink aught until he drink also." "Truly," said the Earl, "it is of no more avail for me to be gentle with thee than ungentle." And he gave her a box in the ear. Thereupon she raised a loud and piercing shriek, and her lamentations were much greater than they had been before, for she considered in her mind that had Geraint been alive, he durst not have struck her thus. But, behold, at the sound of her cry Geraint revived from his swoon, and he sat up on the bier, and finding his sword in the hollow of his shield, he rushed to the place where the Earl was, and struck him a fiercely-wounding, severely-venomous, and sternly-smiting blow upon the crown of his head, so that he clove him in twain, until his sword was stayed by the table. Then all left the board and fled away. And this was not so much through fear of the living as through the dread they felt at seeing the dead man rise up to slay them. And Geraint looked upon Enid, and he was grieved for two causes; one was, to see that Enid had lost her colour and her wonted aspect; and the other, to know that she was in the right. "Lady," said he, "knowest thou where our horses are?" "I know, Lord, where thy horse is," she replied, "but I know not where is the other. Thy horse is in the house yonder." So he went to the house, and brought forth his horse, and mounted him, and took up Enid from the ground, and placed her upon the horse with him. And he rode forward. And their road lay between two hedges. And the night was gaining on the day. And, lo! they saw behind them the shafts of spears betwixt them and the sky, and they heard the trampling of horses, and the noise of a host approaching. "I hear something following us," said he, "and I will put thee on the other side of the hedge." And thus he did. And thereupon, behold, a knight pricked towards him, and couched his lance. When Enid saw this, she cried out, saying, "Oh! chieftain, whoever thou art, what renown wilt thou gain by slaying a dead man?" "Oh! Heaven," said he, "is it Geraint?" "Yes, in truth," said she. "And who art thou?" "I am the Little King," he answered, "coming to thy assistance, for I heard that thou wast in trouble. And if thou hadst followed my advice, none of these hardships would have befallen thee." "Nothing can happen," said Geraint, "without the will of Heaven, though much good results from counsel." "Yes," said the Little King, "and I know good counsel for thee now. Come with me to the court of a son-in-law of my sister, which is near here, and thou shalt have the best medical assistance in the kingdom." "I will do so, gladly," said Geraint. And Enid was placed upon the horse of one of the Little King's squires, and they went forward to the Baron's palace. And they were received there with gladness, and they met with hospitality and attention. And the next morning they went to seek physicians; and it was not long before they came, and they attended Geraint until he was perfectly well. And while Geraint was under medical care, the Little King caused his armour to be repaired, until it was as good as it had ever been. And they remained there a fortnight and a month.

Then the Little King said to Geraint, "Now will we go towards my own Court, to take rest and amuse ourselves." "Not so," said Geraint, "we will first journey for one day more, and return again." "With all my heart," said the Little King, "do thou go then." And early in the day they set forth. And more gladly and more joyfully did Enid journey with them that day than she had ever done. And they came to the main road. And when they reached a place where the road divided in two, they beheld a man on foot coming towards them along one of these roads, and Gwiffert asked the man whence he came. "I come," said he, "from an errand in the country." "Tell me," said Geraint, "which is the best for me to follow of these two roads?" "That is the best for thee to follow," answered he, "for if thou goest by this one, thou wilt never return. Below us," said he, "there is a hedge of mist, and within it are enchanted games, and no one who has gone there has ever returned. And the Court of the Earl Owain is there, and he permits no one to go to lodge in the town except he will go to his Court." "I declare to Heaven," said Geraint, "that we will take the lower road." And they went along it until they came to the town. And they took the fairest and pleasantest place in the town for their lodging. And while they were thus, behold, a young man came to them, and greeted them. "Heaven be propitious to thee," said they. "Good Sirs," said he, "what preparations are you making here?" "We are taking up our lodging," said they, "to pass the night." "It is not the custom with him who owns the town," he answered, "to permit any of gentle birth, unless they come to stay in his Court, to abide here; therefore, come you to the Court." "We will come, gladly," said Geraint. And they went with the page, and they were joyfully received. And the Earl came to the hall to meet them, and he commanded the tables to be laid. And they washed, and sat down. And this is the order in which they sat, Geraint on one side of the Earl, and Enid on the other side, and next to Enid the Little King, and then the Countess next to Geraint, and all after that as became their rank. Then Geraint recollected the games, and thought that he should not go to them; and on that account he did not eat. Then the Earl looked upon Geraint, and considered, and he bethought him that his not eating was because of the games, and it grieved him that he had ever established those games, were it only on account of losing such a youth as Geraint. And if Geraint had asked him to abolish the games, he would gladly have done so. Then the Earl said to Geraint, "What thought occupies thy mind, that thou dost not eat? If thou hesitatest about going to the games, thou shall not go, and no other of thy rank shall ever go either." "Heaven reward thee," said Geraint, "but I wish nothing better than to go to the games, and to be shown the way thither." "If that is what thou dost prefer, thou shalt obtain it willingly." "I do prefer it, indeed," said he. Then they ate, and they were amply served, and they had a variety of gifts, and abundance of liquor. And when they had finished eating, they arose. And Geraint called for his horse and his armour, and he accoutred both himself and his horse. And all the hosts went forth until they came to the side of the hedge, and the hedge was so lofty, that it reached as high as they could see in the air, and upon every stake in the hedge, except two, there was the head of a man, and the number of stakes throughout the hedge was very great. Then said the Little King, "May no one go in with the chieftain?" "No one may," said Earl Owain. "Which way can I enter?" enquired Geraint. "I know not," said Owain, "but enter by the way that thou wilt, and that seemeth easiest to thee."

Then fearlessly and unhesitatingly Geraint dashed forward into the mist. And on leaving the mist he came to a large orchard, and in the orchard he saw an open space, wherein was a tent of red satin, and the door of the tent was open, and an apple-tree stood in front of the door of the tent, and on a branch of the apple-tree hung a huge hunting horn. Then he dismounted, and went into the tent, and there was no one in the tent save one maiden sitting in a golden chair, and another chair was opposite to her, empty. And Geraint went to the empty chair, and sat down therein. "Ah! chieftain," said the maiden, "I would not counsel thee to sit in that chair." "Wherefore?" said Geraint. "The man to whom that chair belongs has never suffered another to sit in it." "I care not," said Geraint, "though it displease him that I sit in the chair." And thereupon they heard a mighty tumult around the tent. And Geraint looked to see what was the cause of the tumult. And he beheld without a knight mounted upon a war-horse, proudly-snorting, high-mettled, and large of bone, and a robe of honour in two parts was upon him and upon his horse, and beneath it was plenty of armour. "Tell me, chieftain," said he to Geraint, "who it was that bade thee sit there?" "Myself," answered he. "It was wrong of thee to do me this shame and disgrace. Arise, and do me satisfaction for thine insolence." Then Geraint arose, and they encountered immediately, and they broke a set of lances; and a second set; and a third; and they gave each other fierce and frequent strokes; and at last Geraint became enraged, and he urged on his horse, and rushed upon him, and gave him a thrust on the centre of his shield, so that it was split, and so that the head of his lance went through his armour, and his girths were broken, and he himself was borne headlong to the ground the length of Geraint's lance and arm, over his horse's crupper. "Oh, my Lord!" said he, "thy mercy, and thou shalt have what thou wilt." "I only desire," said Geraint, "that this game shall no longer exist here, nor the hedge of mist, nor magic, nor enchantment." "Thou shalt have this gladly, Lord," he replied. "Cause then the mist to disappear from this place," said Geraint. "Sound yonder horn," said he, "and when thou soundest it, the mist will vanish; but it will not go hence unless the horn be blown by the knight by whom I am vanquished." And sad and sorrowful was Enid where she remained, through anxiety concerning Geraint. Then Geraint went and sounded the horn. And at the first blast he gave, the mist vanished. And all the hosts came together, and they all became reconciled to each other. And the Earl invited Geraint and the Little King to stay with him that night. And the next morning they separated. And Geraint went towards his own dominions; and thenceforth he reigned prosperously, and his warlike fame and splendour lasted with renown and honour both to him and to Enid from that time forward.

KILHWCH AND OLWEN
OR THE
TWRCH TRWYTH

Kilydd, the son of Prince Kelyddon desired a wife as a helpmate, and the wife that he chose was Goleuddydd, the daughter of Prince Anlawdd. And after their union the people put up prayers that they might have an heir. And they had a son through the prayers of the people. From the time of her pregnancy Goleuddydd became wild, and wandered about, without habitation; but when her delivery was at hand, her reason came back to her. Then she went to a mountain where there was a swineherd, keeping a herd of swine. And through fear of the swine the queen was delivered. And the swineherd took the boy, and brought him to the palace; and he was christened, and they called him Kilhwch, because he had been found in a swine's burrow. Nevertheless the boy was of gentle lineage, and cousin unto Arthur; and they put him out to nurse.

After this the boy's mother, Goleuddydd, the daughter of Prince Anlawdd, fell sick. Then she called her husband unto her, and said to him, "Of this sickness I shall die, and thou wilt take another wife. Now wives are the gift of the Lord, but it would be wrong for thee to harm thy son. Therefore I charge thee that thou take not a wife until thou see a briar with two blossoms upon my grave." And this he promised her. Then she besought him to dress her grave every year, that nothing might grow thereon. [64] So the queen died. Now the king sent an attendant every morning to see if anything were growing upon the grave. And at the end of the seventh year the master neglected that which he had promised to the queen.

One day the king went to hunt, and he rode to the place of burial, to see the grave, and to know if it were time that he should take a wife; and the king saw the briar. And when he saw it, the king took counsel where he should find a wife. Said one of his counsellors, "I know a wife that will suit thee well, and she is the wife of King Doged." And they resolved to go to seek her; and they slew the king, and brought away his wife and one daughter that she had along with her. And they conquered the king's lands.

On a certain day as the lady walked abroad, she came to the house of an old crone that dwelt in the town, and that had no tooth in her head. And the queen said to her, "Old woman, tell me that which I shall ask thee, for the love of Heaven. Where are the children of the man who has carried me away by violence?" Said the crone, "He has not children." Said the queen, "Woe is me, that I should have come to one who is childless!" Then said the hag, "Thou needest not lament on account of that, for there is a prediction that he shall have an heir by thee, and by none other. Moreover, be not sorrowful, for he has one son."

The lady returned home with joy, and she asked her consort, "Wherefore hast thou concealed thy children from me?" The king said, "I will do so no longer." And he sent messengers for his son, and he was brought to the Court. His stepmother said unto him, "It were well for thee to have a wife, and I have a daughter who is sought of every man of renown in the world." "I am not yet of an age to wed," answered the youth. Then said she unto him, "I declare to thee, that it is thy destiny not to be suited with a wife until thou obtain Olwen, the daughter of Yspaddaden Penkawr." And the youth blushed, and the love of the maiden diffused itself through all his frame, although he had never seen her. And his father enquired of him, "What has come over thee, my son, and what aileth thee?" "My stepmother has declared to me, that I shall never have a wife until I obtain Olwen, the daughter of Yspaddaden Penkawr." "That will be easy for thee," answered his father. "Arthur is thy cousin. Go, therefore, unto Arthur, to cut thy hair, and ask this of him as a boon."

And the youth pricked forth upon a steed with head dappled grey, of four winters old, firm of limb, with shell-formed hoofs, having a bridle of linked gold on his head, and upon him a saddle of costly gold. And in the youth's hand were two spears of silver, sharp, well-tempered, headed with steel, three ells in length, of an edge to wound the wind, and cause blood to flow, and swifter than the fall [66] of the dew-drop from the blade of reed grass upon the earth, when the dew of June is at the heaviest. A gold-hilted sword was upon his thigh, the blade of which was of gold, bearing a cross of inlaid gold of the hue of the lightning of heaven: his war-horn was of ivory. Before him were two brindled white-breasted greyhounds, having strong collars of rubies about their necks, reaching from the shoulder to the ear. And the one that was on the left side bounded across to the right side, and the one on the right to the left, and like two sea swallows sported around him. And his courser cast up four sods with his four hoofs, like four swallows in the air, about his head, now above, now below. About him was a four-cornered cloth of purple, and an apple of gold was at each corner; and every one of the apples was of the value of an hundred kine. And there was precious gold of the value of three hundred kine upon his shoes, and upon his stirrups, from his knee to the tip of his toe. And the blade of grass bent not beneath him, so light was his courser's tread as he journeyed towards the gate of Arthur's palace.

Spoke the youth, "Is there a porter?" "There is; and if thou holdest not thy peace, small will be thy welcome. [67] I am Arthur's porter every first day of January. And during every other part of the year but this the office is filled by Huandaw, and Gogigwc, and Llaeskenym, and Pennpingyon, who goes upon his head to save his feet, neither towards the sky nor towards the earth, but like a rolling stone upon the floor of the Court." "Open the portal." "I will not open it." "Wherefore not?" "The knife is in the meat, and the drink is in the horn, and there is revelry in Arthur's hall, and none may enter therein but the son of a king of a privileged country, or a craftsman bringing his craft. But there will be refreshment for thy dogs, and for thy horses; and for thee there will be collops cooked and peppered, and luscious wine and mirthful songs, and food for fifty men shall be brought unto thee in the guest chamber, where the stranger and the sons of other countries eat, who come not unto the precincts of the Palace of Arthur. Thou wilt fare no worse there than thou wouldest with Arthur in the Court. A lady shall smooth thy couch, and shall lull thee with songs; and early to-morrow morning, when the gate is open for the multitude that came hither to-day, for thee shall it be opened first, and thou mayest sit in the place that thou shall choose in Arthur's Hall, from the upper end to the lower." Said the youth, "That will I not do. If thou openest the gate, it is well. If thou dost not open it, I will bring disgrace upon thy Lord, and evil report upon thee. And I will set up three shouts at this very gate, than which none were ever more deadly, from the top of Pengwaed in Cornwall to the bottom of Dinsol, in the North, and to Esgair Oervel, in Ireland. And all the women in this Palace that are pregnant shall lose their offspring; and such as are not pregnant, their hearts shall be turned by illness, so that they shall never bear children from this day forward." "What clamour soever thou mayest make," said Glewlwyd Gavaelvawr, "against the laws of Arthur's Palace, shalt thou not enter therein, until I first go and speak with Arthur." Then Glewlwyd went into the Hall. And Arthur said to him, "Hast thou news from the gate?"—"Half of my life is past, and half of thine. I was heretofore in Kaer Se and Asse, in Sach and Salach, in Lotor and Fotor; and I have been heretofore in India the Great and India the Lesser; and I was in the battle of Dau Ynyr, when the twelve hostages were brought from Llychlyn. And I have also been in Europe, and in Africa, and in the Islands of Corsica, and in Caer Brythwch, and Brythach, and Verthach; and I was present when formerly thou didst slay the family of Clis the son of Merin, and when thou didst slay Mil Du, the son of Ducum, and when thou didst conquer Greece in the East. And I have been in Caer Oeth and Annoeth, and in Caer Nevenhyr; nine supreme sovereigns, handsome men, saw we there, but never did I behold a man of equal dignity with him who is now at the door of the portal." Then said Arthur, "If walking thou didst enter in here, return thou running. And every one that beholds the light, and every one that opens and shuts the eye, let him show him respect, and serve him, some with gold-mounted drinking horns, others with collops cooked and peppered, until food and drink can be prepared for him. It is unbecoming to keep such a man as thou sayest he is in the wind and the rain." Said Kai, "By the hand of my friend, if thou wouldest follow my counsel, thou wouldest not break through the laws of the Court because of him." "Not so, blessed Kai, it is an honour to us to be resorted to, and the greater our courtesy, the greater will be our renown, and our fame, and our glory."

And Glewlwyd came to the gate, and opened the gate before him; and although all dismounted upon the horse-block at the gate, yet did he not dismount, but he rode in upon his charger. Then said Kilhwch, "Greeting be unto thee, Sovereign Ruler of this Island; and be this greeting no less unto the lowest than unto the highest, and be it equally unto thy guests, and thy warriors, and thy chieftains—let all partake of it as completely as thyself. And complete be thy favour, and thy fame, and thy glory, throughout all this Island." "Greeting unto thee also," said Arthur, "sit thou between two of my warriors, and thou shalt have minstrels before thee, and thou shalt enjoy the privileges of a king born to a throne, as long as thou remainest here. And when I dispense my presents to the visitors and strangers in this Court, they shall be in thy hand at my commencing." Said the youth, "I came not here to consume meat and drink; but if I obtain the boon that I seek, I will requite it thee, and extol thee; and if I have it not, I will bear forth thy dispraise to the four quarters of the world, as far as thy renown has extended." Then said Arthur, "Since thou wilt not remain here, chieftain, thou shalt receive the boon whatsoever thy tongue may name, as far as the wind dries and the rain moistens, and the sun revolves, and the sea encircles, and the earth extends; save only my ship; and my mantle; and Caledvwlch, my sword, and Rhongomyant, my lance; and Wynebgwrthucher, my shield; and Carnwenhau, [70a] my dagger; and Gwenhwyvar, my wife. By the truth of Heaven, thou shalt have it cheerfully, name what thou wilt." "I would that thou bless [70b] my hair." "That shalt be granted thee."

And Arthur took a golden comb, and scissors, whereof the loops were of silver, and he combed his hair. And Arthur enquired of him who he was. "For my heart warms unto thee, and I know that thou art come of my blood. Tell me, therefore, who thou art." "I will tell thee," said the youth, "I am Kilhwch, the son of Kilydd, the son of Prince Kelyddon, by Goleuddydd, my mother, the daughter of Prince Anlawdd." "That is true," said Arthur. "Thou art my cousin. Whatsoever boon thou mayest ask, thou shalt receive, be it what it may that thy tongue shall name." "Pledge the truth of Heaven and the faith of thy kingdom thereof." "I pledge it thee, gladly." "I crave of thee then, that thou obtain for me Olwen, the daughter of Yspaddaden Penkawr, and this boon I likewise seek at the hands of thy warriors. I seek it from Kai, and Bedwyr, and Greidawl Galldonyd, [71a] and Gwythyr the son of Greidawl, and Greid the son of Eri, and Kynddelig Kyvarwydd, and Tathal Twyll Goleu, and Maelwys the son of Baeddan, and Crychwr [71b] the son of Nes, and Cubert the son of Daere, and Percos the son of Poch, and Lluber Beuthach, and Corvil Bervach, and Gwynn the son of Nudd, and Edeyrn the son of Nudd, and Gadwy [71c] the son of Geraint, and Prince Fflewddur Fflam, and Ruawn Pebyr the son of Dorath, and Bradwen the son of Moren Mynawc, and Moren Mynawc himself, and Dalldav the son of Kimin Côv, and the son of Alun Dyved, and the son of Saidi, and the son of Gwryon, and Uchtryd Ardywad Kad, and Kynwas Curvagyl, and Gwrhyr Gwarthegvras, and Isperyr Ewingath, and Gallcoyt Govynynat, and Duach, and Grathach, and Nerthach, the sons of Gwawrddur Kyrvach, (these men came forth from the confines of Hell), and Kilydd Canhastyr, and Canastyr Kanllaw, and Cors Cant-Ewin, and Esgeir Gulhwch Govynkawn, and Drustwrn Hayarn, and Glewlwyd Gavaelvawr, and Lloch Llawwynnyawc, and Aunwas [71d] Adeiniawc, and Sinnoch the son of Seithved, and Gwennwynwyn the son of Naw, and Bedyw the son of Seithved, and Gobrwy the son of Echel Vorddwyttwll, and Echel Vorddwyttwll himself, and Mael the son of Roycol, and Dadweir Dallpenn, and Garwyli the son of Gwythawc Gwyr, and Gwythawc Gwyr himself, and Gormant the son of Ricca, and Menw the son of Teirgwaedd, and Digon the son of Alar, and Selyf the son of Smoit, [71e] and Gusg the son of Atheu, and Nerth the son of Kedarn, and Drudwas the son of Tryffin, and Twrch the son of Perif, and Twrch the son of Annwas, and Iona king of France, and Sel the son of Selgi, and Teregud the son of Iaen, and Sulyen the son of Iaen, and Bradwen the son of Iaen, and Moren the son of Iaen, and Siawn the son of Iaen, and Cradawc the son of Iaen. (They were men of Caerdathal, of Arthur's kindred on his father's side.) Dirmyg the son of Kaw, and Justic the son of Kaw, and Etmic the son of Kaw, and Anghawd the son of Kaw, and Ovan the son of Kaw, and Kelin the son of Kaw, and Connyn the son of Kaw, and Mabsant the son of Kaw, and Gwyngad the son of Kaw, and Llwybyr the son of Kaw, and Coth the son of Kaw, and Meilic the son of Kaw, and Kynwas the son of Kaw, and Ardwyad the son of Kaw, and Ergyryad the son of Kaw, and Neb the son of Kaw, and Gilda the son of Kaw, and Calcas the son of Kaw, and Hueil the son of Kaw, (he never yet made a request at the hand of any Lord). And Samson Vinsych, and Taliesin the chief of the bards, and Mamawyddan the son of Llyr, and Llary the son of Prince Kasnar, and Ysperni [72a] the son of Fflergant king of Armorica, and Saranhon the son of Glythwyr, and Llawr Eilerw, and Annyanniawc the son of Menw the son of Teirgwaedd, and Gwynn the son of Nwyvre, and Fflam the son of Nwyvre, and Geraint the son of Erbin, and Ermid [72b] the son of Erbin, and Dyvel the son of Erbin, and Gwynn the son of Ermid, and Kyndrwyn the son of Ermid, and Hyveidd Unllenn, and Eiddon Vawr Vrydic, and Reidwn Arwy, and Gormant the son of Ricca (Arthur's brother by his mother's side; the Penhynev of Cornwall was his father), and Llawnrodded Varvawc, and Nodawl Varyf Twrch, and Berth the son of Kado, and Rheidwn the son of Beli, and Iscovan Hael, and Iscawin the son of Panon, and Morvran the son of Tegid (no one struck him in the battle of Camlan by reason of his ugliness; all thought he was an auxiliary devil. Hair had he upon him like the hair of a stag). And Sandde Bryd Angel (no one touched him with a spear in the battle of Camlan because of his beauty; all thought he was a ministering angel). And Kynwyl Sant, the third man that escaped from the battle of Camlan, (and he was the last who parted from Arthur on Hengroen his horse). And Uchtryd the son of Erim, and Eus the son of Erim, and Henwas Adeinawg the son of Erim, and Henbedestyr the son of Erim, and Sgilti Yscawndroed son of Erim. (Unto these three men belonged these three qualities,—with Henbedestyr there was not any one who could keep pace, either on horseback or on foot; with Henwas Adeinawg, no four-footed beast could run the distance of an acre, much less could it go beyond it; and as to Sgilti Yscawndroed, when he intended to go upon a message for his Lord, he never sought to find a path, but knowing whither he was to go, if his way lay through a wood he went along the tops of the trees. During his whole life, a blade of reed grass bent not beneath his feet, much less did one ever break, so lightly did he tread.) Teithi Hên the son of Gwynhan, (his dominions were swallowed up by the sea and he himself hardly escaped, and he came to Arthur; and his knife had this peculiarity, that from the time that he came there, no haft would ever remain upon it, and owing to this a sickness came over him, and he pined away during the remainder of his life, and of this he died). And Carneddyr the son of Govynyon Hên, and Gwenwynwyn the son of Nav Gyssevin, Arthur's champion, and Llysgadrudd Emys, and Gwrbothu Hên, (uncles unto Arthur were they, his mother's brothers). Kulvanawyd the son of Goryon, and Llenlleawg [74a] Wyddel from the headland of Ganion, and Dyvynwal Moel, and Dunard king of the North, Teirnon Twryf Bliant, and Tegvan Gloff, and Tegyr Talgellawg, Gwrdinal [74b] the son of Ebrei, and Morgant Hael, Gwystyl the son of Rhun the son of Nwython, and Llwyddeu, the son of Nwython, and Gwydre the son of Llwyddeu, (Gwenabwy the daughter of [Kaw] was his mother, Hueil his uncle stabbed him, and hatred was between Hueil and Arthur because of the wound). Drem the son of Dremidyd, (when the gnat arose in the morning with the sun, he could see it from Gelli Wic in Cornwall, as far off as Pen Blathaon in North Britain). And Eidyol the son of Ner, and Glwyddyn Saer, (who constructed Ehangwen, Arthur's Hall). Kynyr Keinvarvawc, (when he was told he had a son born, [74c] he said to his wife, 'Damsel, if thy son be mine, his heart will be always cold, and there will be no warmth in his hands; and he will have another peculiarity, if he is my son he will always be stubborn; and he will have another peculiarity, when he carries a burden, whether it be large or small, no one will be able to see it, either before him or at his back; and he will have another peculiarity, no one will be able to resist water and fire so well as he will; and he will have another peculiarity, there will never be a servant or an officer equal to him'). Henwas, and Henwyneb, (an old companion to Arthur). Gwallgoyc, (another; when he came to a town, though there were three hundred houses in it, if he wanted any thing, he would not let sleep come to the eyes of any one whilst he remained there). Berwyn the son of Gerenhir, and Paris king of France, [75a] and Osla Gyllellvawr, (who bore a short broad dagger. When Arthur and his hosts came before a torrent, they would seek for a narrow place where they might pass the water, and would lay the sheathed dagger across the torrent, and it would form a bridge sufficient for the armies of the three Islands of Britain, and of the three Islands adjacent, with their spoil). Gwyddawg the son of Menestyr, (who slew Kai, and whom Arthur slew together with his brothers, to revenge Kai). Garanwyn the son of Kai, and Amren the son of Bedwyr, and Ely Amyr, and Rheu Rhwyd Dyrys, and Rhun Rhudwern, and Eli, and Trachmyr, (Arthur's chief huntsmen). And Llwyddeu the son of Kelcoed, and Hunabwy the son of Gwryon, and Gwynn Godyvron, and Gweir Datharwenniddawg, and Gweir the son of Cadell the son of Talaryant, [75b] and Gweir Gwrhyd Ennwir, and Gweir Paladyr Hir, (the uncles of Arthur, the brothers of his mother). The sons of Llwch Llawwynnyawg, (from beyond the raging sea). Llenlleawg Wyddel, and Ardderchawg Prydain. Cas the son of Saidi, Gwrvan Gwallt Avwyn, and Gwyllennhin the king of France, and Gwittart the son of Oedd king of Ireland, Garselit Wyddel, Panawr Pen Bagad, and Ffleudor the son of Nav, Gwynnhyvar mayor of Cornwall and Devon, (the ninth man that rallied the battle of Camlan). Keli and Kueli, and Gilla Coes Hydd, (he would clear three hundred acres at one bound. The chief leaper of Ireland was he). Sol, and Gwadyn Ossol and Gwadyn Odyeith. (Sol could stand all day upon one foot. Gwadyn Ossol, if he stood upon the top of the highest mountain in the world, it would become a level plain under his feet. Gwadyn Odyeith, the soles of his feet emitted sparks of fire when they struck upon things hard, like the heated mass when drawn out of the forge. He cleared the way for Arthur when he came to any stoppage.) Hirerwm and Hiratrwm. (The day they went on a visit three Cantrevs provided for their entertainment, and they feasted until noon and drank until night, when they went to sleep. And then they devoured the heads of the vermin through hunger, as if they had never eaten anything. When they made a visit, they left neither the fat nor the lean, neither the hot nor the cold, the sour nor the sweet, the fresh nor the salt, the boiled nor the raw.) Huarwar the son of Aflawn, (who asked Arthur such a boon as would satisfy him. It was the third great plague of Cornwall when he received it. None could get a smile from him but when he was satisfied). Gware Gwallt Euryn. The two cubs of Gast Rhymi, Gwyddrud and Gwyddneu Astrus. Sugyn the son of Sugnedydd, (who would suck up the sea on which were three hundred ships, so as to leave nothing but a dry strand. He was broad-chested). [76a] Rhacymwri, the attendant of Arthur; (whatever barn he was shown, were there the produce of thirty ploughs within it, he would strike it with an iron flail until the rafters, the beams, and the boards, were no better than the small oats in the mow upon the floor of the barn). Dygyflwng, and Anoeth Veidawg. And Hir Eiddyl, and Hir Amreu, (they were two attendants of Arthur). And Gwevyl the son of Gwestad, (on the day that he was sad, he would let one of his lips drop below his waist, while he turned up the other like a cap upon his head). Uchtryd Varyf Draws, (who spread his red untrimmed beard over the eight-and-forty rafters which were in Arthur's Hall). Elidyr Gyvarwydd, Yskyrdav, and Yscudydd, (two attendants of Gwenhwyvar were they. Their feet were swift as their thoughts when bearing a message). Brys the son of Bryssethach, (from the Hill of the Black Fernbrake in North Britain). And Grudlwyn Gorr. Bwlch, and Kyfwlch, and Sefwlch, the sons of Cleddyf Kyfwlch, the grandsons of Cleddyf Difwlch. (Their three shields were three gleaming glitterers; their three spears were three pointed piercers; their three swords were three griding gashers; Glas, Glessic, and Gleisad. Their three dogs, Call, Cuall, and Cavall. Their three horses, Hwyrdyddwd, and Drwgdyddwd, and Llwyrdyddwg. [77a] Their three wives, Och, and Garym, and Diaspad. Their three grand-children, Lluched, and Neved, and Eissiwed. Their three daughters, Drwg, and Gwaeth, and Gwaethav Oll. Their three handmaids, Eheubryd the daughter of Kyfwlch, Gorascwrn the daughter of Nerth, Ewaedan the daughter of Kynvelyn Keudawd Pwyll the half man.) Dwnn Diessic Unbenn, Eiladyr the son of Pen Llarcau, Kynedyr Wyllt the son of Hettwn Talaryant, Sawyl, Ben Uchel, Gwalchmai the son of Gwyar, Gwalhaved the son of Gwyar, Gwrhyr Gwastawd Ieithoedd, (to whom all tongues were known,) and Kethcrwn [77b] the Priest. Clust the son of Clustveinad, (though he were buried seven cubits beneath the earth, he would hear the ant, fifty miles off, rise from her nest in the morning). Medyr the son of Methredydd, (from Gelli Wic he could, in a twinkling, shoot the wren through the two legs upon Esgeir Oervel in Ireland). Gwiawn Llygad Cath, (who would cut a haw from the eye of the gnat without hurting him). Ol the son of Olwydd; (seven years before he was born his father's swine were carried off, and when he grew up a man, he tracked the swine, and brought them back in seven herds). Bedwini the Bishop, (who blessed Arthur's meat and drink). For the sake of the golden-chained daughters of this island. For the sake of Gwenhwyvar, its chief lady, and Gwennhwyach her sister, and Rathtyeu the only daughter of Clemenhill, and Rhelemon the daughter of Kai, and Tannwen the daughter of Gweir Datharwenîddawg. [78a] Gwenn Alarch, the daughter of Kynwyl Canbwch. [78b] Eurneid the daughter of Clydno Eiddin. Eneuawc the daughter of Bedwyr. Enrydreg the daughter of Tudvathar. Gwennwledyr the daughter of Gwaledyr Kyrvach. Erddudnid the daughter of Tryffin. Eurolwen the daughter of Gwdolwyn Gorr. Teleri the daughter of Peul. Indeg the daughter of Garwy [78c] Hir. Morvudd the daughter of Urien Rheged. Gwenllian Deg the majestic maiden. Creiddylad the daughter of Llud Llaw Ereint. (She was the most splendid maiden in the three Islands of the mighty, and in the three

Islands adjacent, and for her Gwythyr the son of Greidawl and Gwynn the son of Nudd fight every first of May until the day of doom.) Ellylw the daughter of Neol Kynn-Crog. (She lived three ages.) Essyllt Vinwen, and Essyllt Vingul." And all these did Kilhwch son of Kilydd adjure to obtain his boon.

Then said Arthur, "Oh! Chieftain, I have never heard of the maiden of whom thou speakest, nor of her kindred, but I will gladly send messengers in search of her. Give me time to seek her." And the youth said, "I will willingly grant from this night to that at the end of the year to do so." Then Arthur sent messengers to every land within his dominions, to seek for the maiden, and at the end of the year Arthur's messengers returned without having gained any knowledge or intelligence concerning Olwen, more than on the first day. Then said Kilhwch, "Every one has received his boon, and I yet lack mine. I will depart and bear away thy honour with me." Then said Kai, "Rash chieftain! dost thou reproach Arthur? Go with us, and we will not part until thou dost either confess that the maiden exists not in the world, or until we obtain her." Thereupon Kai rose up. Kai had this peculiarity, that his breath lasted nine nights and nine days under water, and he could exist nine nights and nine days without sleep. A wound from Kai's sword no physician could heal. Very subtle was Kai. When it pleased him he could render himself as tall as the highest tree in the forest. And he had another peculiarity,—so great was the heat of his nature, that when it rained hardest, whatever he carried remained dry for a handbreadth above and a handbreadth below his hand; and when his companions were coldest, it was to them as fuel with which to light their fire.

And Arthur called Bedwyr, who never shrank from any enterprise upon which Kai was bound. None were equal to him in swiftness throughout this Island except Arthur and Drych Ail Kibddar. And although he was one-handed, three warriors could not shed blood faster than he on the field of battle. Another property he had, his lance would produce a wound equal to those of nine opposing lances.

And Arthur called to Kynddelig the Guide, "Go thou upon this expedition with the chieftain." For as good a guide was he in a land which he had never seen as he was in his own.

He called Gwrhyr Gwalstawt Ieithoedd, because he knew all tongues.

He called Gwalchmai the son of Gwyar, because he never returned home without achieving the adventure of which he went in quest. He was the best of footmen and the best of knights. He was nephew to Arthur, the son of his sister, and his cousin.

And Arthur called Menw the son of Teirgwaedd, in order that if they went into a savage country, he might cast a charm and an illusion over them, so that none might see them, whilst they could see every one.

They journeyed until they came to a vast open plain, wherein they saw a great castle, which was the fairest of the castles of the world. And they journeyed that day until the evening, and when they thought they were nigh to the castle, they were no nearer to it than they had been in the morning. And the second and the third day they journeyed, and even then scarcely could they reach so far. And when they came before the castle, they beheld a vast flock of sheep, which was boundless, and without an end. And upon the top of a mound there was a herdsman, keeping the sheep. And a rug made of skins was upon him; and by his side was a shaggy mastiff, larger than a steed nine winters old. Never had he lost even a lamb from his flock, much less a large sheep. He let no occasion ever pass without doing some hurt and harm. All the dead trees and bushes in the plain he burnt with his breath down to the very ground.

Then said Kai, "Gwrhyr Gwalstawt Ieithoedd, go thou and salute yonder man." "Kai," said he, "I engaged not to go further than thou thyself." "Let us go then together," answered Kai. [81a] Said Menw the son of Teirgwaedd, "Fear not to go thither, for I will cast a spell upon the dog, so that he shall injure no one." And they went up to the mound whereon the herdsman was, and they said to him, "How dost thou fare? O herdsman!" "No less fair be it to you than to me." "Truly, art thou the chief?" "There is no hurt to injure me but my own." [81b] "Whose are the sheep that thou dost keep, and to whom does yonder castle belong?" "Stupid are ye, truly! Through the whole world is it known that this is the castle of Yspaddaden Penkawr." "And who art thou?" "I am called Custennin the son of Dyfnedig, and my brother Yspaddaden Penkawr oppressed me because of my possession. And ye also, who are ye?" "We are an embassy from Arthur, come to seek Olwen, the daughter of Yspaddaden Penkawr." "Oh men! the mercy of Heaven be upon you, do not that for all the world. None who ever came hither on this quest has returned alive." And the herdsman rose up. And as he arose, Kilhwch gave unto him a ring of gold. And he sought to put on the ring, but it was too small for him, so he placed it in the finger of his glove. And he went home, and gave the glove to his spouse to keep. And she took the ring from the glove when it was given her, and she said, "Whence came this ring, for thou art not wont to have good fortune?" "I went," said he, "to the sea to seek for fish, and lo, I saw a corpse borne by the waves. And a fairer corpse than it did I never behold. And from its finger did I take this ring." "Oh man! does the sea permit its dead to wear jewels? Show me then this body." "Oh wife, him to whom this ring belonged thou shalt see herein the evening." [82] "And who is he?" asked the woman. "Kilhwch the son of

Kilydd, the son of Prince Kelyddon, by Goleuddydd the daughter of Prince Anlawdd, his mother, who is come to seek Olwen as his wife." And when she heard that, her feelings were divided between the joy that she had that her nephew, the son of her sister, was coming to her, and sorrow because she had never known any one depart alive who had come on that quest.

And they went forward to the gate of Custennin the herdsman's dwelling. And when she heard their footsteps approaching, she ran out with joy to meet them. And Kai snatched a billet out of the pile. And when she met them she sought to throw her arms about their necks. And Kai placed the log between her two hands, and she squeezed it so that it became a twisted coil. "Oh woman," said Kai, "if thou hadst squeezed me thus, none could ever again have set their affections on me. Evil love were this." They entered into the house, and were served; and soon after they all went forth to amuse themselves. Then the woman opened a stone chest that was before the chimney corner, and out of it arose a youth with yellow curling hair. Said Gwrhyr, "It is a pity to hide this youth. I know that it is not his own crime that is thus visited upon him." "This is but a remnant," said the woman. "Three and twenty of my sons has Yspaddaden Penkawr slain, and I have no more hope of this one than of the others." Then said Kai, "Let him come and be a companion with me, and he shall not be slain unless I also am slain with him." And they ate. And the woman asked them, "Upon what errand come you here?" "We come to seek Olwen for this youth." Then said the woman, "In the name of Heaven, since no one from the castle hath yet seen you, return again whence you came." "Heaven is our witness, that we will not return until we have seen the maiden." Said Kai, "Does she ever come hither, so that she may be seen?" "She comes here every Saturday to wash her head, and in the vessel where she washes, she leaves all her rings, and she never either comes herself or sends any messengers to fetch them." "Will she come here if she is sent to?" "Heaven knows that I will not destroy my soul, nor will I betray those that trust me; unless you will pledge me your faith that you will not harm her, I will not send to her." "We pledge it," said they. So a message was sent, and she came.

The maiden was clothed in a robe of flame-coloured silk, and about her neck was a collar of ruddy gold, on which were precious emeralds and rubies. More yellow was her head than the flower of the broom, and her skin was whiter than the foam of the wave, and fairer were her hands and her fingers than the blossoms of the wood anemone amidst the spray of the meadow fountain. The eye of the trained hawk, the glance of the three-mewed falcon, was not brighter than hers. Her bosom was more snowy than the breast of the white swan, her cheek was redder than the reddest roses. Whoso beheld her was filled with her love. Four white trefoils sprung up wherever she trod. And therefore was she called Olwen.

She entered the house, and sat beside Kilhwch upon the foremost bench; and as soon as he saw her he knew her. And Kilhwch said unto her, "Ah! maiden, thou art she whom I have loved; come away with me lest they speak evil of thee and of me. Many a day have I loved thee." "I cannot do this, for I have pledged my faith to my father not to go without his counsel, for his life will last only until the time of my espousals. Whatever is, must be. But I will give thee advice if thou wilt take it. Go, ask me of my father, and that which he shall require of thee, grant it, and thou wilt obtain me; but if thou deny him anything, thou wilt not obtain me, and it will be well for thee if thou escape with thy life." "I promise all this, if occasion offer," said he. [84a]

She returned to her chamber, and they all rose up and followed her to the castle. And they slew the nine porters that were at the nine gates in silence. And they slew the nine watch-dogs without one of them barking. And they went forward to the hall.

"The greeting of Heaven and of man be unto thee, Yspaddaden Penkawr," said they. "And you, wherefore come you?" "We come to ask thy daughter Olwen, for Kilhwch the son of Kilydd, the son of Prince Kelyddon." "Where are my pages and my servants? [84b] Raise up the forks beneath my two eyebrows which have fallen over my eyes, that I may see the fashion of my son-in-law." And they did so. "Come hither to-morrow, and you shall have an answer."

They rose to go forth, and Yspaddaden Penkawr seized one of the three poisoned darts that lay beside him, and threw it after them. And Bedwyr caught it, and flung it, and pierced Yspaddaden Penkawr grievously with it through the knee. [85a] Then he said, "A cursed ungentle son-in-law, truly. I shall ever walk the worse for his rudeness, and shall ever be without a cure. This poisoned iron pains me like the bite of a gad-fly. Cursed be the smith who forged it, and the anvil whereon it was wrought! So sharp is it!"

That night also they took up their abode in the house of Custennin the herdsman. The next day with the dawn, they arrayed themselves in haste, and proceeded to the castle, and entered the hall, and they said, "Yspaddaden Penkawr, give us thy daughter in consideration of her dower and her maiden fee, which we will pay to thee and to her two kinswomen likewise. And unless thou wilt do so, thou shall meet with thy death on her account." Then he said, "Her four great-grandmothers, and her four great-grandsires are yet alive, it is needful that I take counsel of them." "Be it so," answered they, "we will go to meat." As they rose up; he took the second dart that was beside him, and cast it after them. And Menw the son of Gwaedd caught it, and flung it back at him, and wounded him in the centre of the breast, so that it came out at the small of his back. "A cursed ungentle son-in-law, truly," said he, "the hard iron pains me like the bite of a horse-leech. Cursed be the hearth whereon it was heated, and the smith who formed it! So sharp is it! Henceforth, whenever I go up a hill, I shall have a scant in my breath, and a pain in my chest, and I shall often loathe my food." And they went to meat.

And the third day they returned to the palace. And Yspaddaden Penkawr said to them, "Shoot not at me again unless you desire death. Where are my attendants? Lift up the forks of my eyebrows which have fallen over my eyeballs, that I may see the fashion of my son-in-law." Then they arose, and, as they did so, Yspaddaden Penkawr took the third poisoned dart, and cast it at them. And Kilhwch caught it, and threw it vigorously, and wounded him through the eyeball, so that the dart came out at the back of his head. "A cursed ungentle son-in-law, truly! As long as I remain alive, my eyesight will be the worse. Whenever I go against the wind, my eyes will water; and peradventure my head will burn, and I shall have a giddiness every new moon. Cursed be the fire in which it was forged. Like the bite of a mad dog is the stroke of this poisoned iron." And they went to meat.

And the next day they came again to the palace, and they said, "Shoot not at us any more, unless thou desirest such hurt, and harm, and torture as thou now hast, and even more. Give me thy daughter; and if thou wilt not give her, thou shall receive thy death because of her." "Where is he that seeks my daughter? Come hither where I may see thee." And they placed him a chair face to face with him.

Said Yspaddaden Penkawr, "Is it thou that seekest my daughter?" "It is I," answered Kilhwch. "I must have thy pledge that thou wilt not do towards me otherwise than is just, and, when I have gotten that which I shall name, my daughter thou shalt have." "I promise thee that willingly," said Kilhwch; "name what thou wilt." "I will do so," said he.

"Seest thou yonder vast hill?" "I see it." "I require that it be rooted up, and that the grubbings be burned for manure on the face of the land, and that it be ploughed and sown in one day, and in one day that the grain ripen. And of that wheat I intend to make food and liquor fit for the wedding of thee and my daughter. And all this I require to be done in one day."

"It will be easy for me to compass this, although thou mayest think that it will not be easy."

"Though this be easy for thee, there is yet that which will not be so. No husbandman can till or prepare this land, so wild is it, except Amaethon the son of Don, and he will not come with thee by his own free will, and thou wilt not be able to compel him."

"It will be easy for me to compass this, although thou mayest think that it will not be easy."

"Though thou get this, there is yet that which thou wilt not get. Govannon the son of Don to come to the headland to rid the iron, he will do no work of his own good will except for a lawful king, and thou wilt not be able to compel him." "It will be easy for me to compass this." "Though thou get this, there is yet that which thou wilt not get; the two dun oxen of Gwlwlyd, [87] both yoked together, to plough the wild land yonder stoutly. He will not give them of his own free will, and thou wilt not be able to compel him." "It will be easy for me to compass this." "Though thou get this, there is yet that which thou wilt not get; the yellow and the brindled bull yoked together do I require."

"It will be easy for me to compass this."

"Though thou get this, there is yet that which thou wilt not get; the two horned oxen, one of which is beyond, and the other this side of the peaked mountain, yoked together in the same plough. And these are Nynniaw and Peibaw, whom God turned into oxen on account of their sins."

"It will be easy for me to compass this."

"Though thou get this, there is yet that which thou wilt not get. Seest thou yonder red tilled ground?"

"I see it."

"When first I met the mother of this maiden, nine bushels of flax were sown therein, and none has yet sprung up, neither white nor black; and I have the measure by me still. I require to have the flax to sow in the new land yonder, that when it grows up it may make a white wimple, for my daughter's head on the day of thy wedding."

"It will be easy for me to compass this, although thou mayest think that it will not be easy."

"Though thou get this, there is yet that which thou wilt not get. Honey that is nine times sweeter than the honey of the virgin swarm, without scum and bees, do I require to make bragget for the feast."

"It will be easy for me to compass this, although thou mayest think that it will not be easy."

"The vessel of Llwyr the son of Llwyryon, which is of the utmost value. There is no other vessel in the world that can hold this drink. Of his free will thou wilt not get it, and thou canst not compel him."

"It will be easy for me to compass this, although thou mayest think that it will not be easy."

"Though thou get this, there is yet that which thou wilt not get. The basket of Gwyddneu Garanhir, if the whole world should come together, thrice nine men at a time, the meat that each of them desired would be found within it. I require to eat therefrom on the night that my daughter becomes thy bride. He will give it to no one of his own free will, and thou canst not compel him."

"It will be easy for me to compass this, although thou mayest think that it will not be easy."

"Though thou get this, there is yet that which thou wilt not get. The horn of Gwlgawd Gododin to serve us with liquor that night. He will not give it of his own free will, and thou wilt not be able to compel him."

"It will be easy for me to compass this, although thou mayest think that it will not be easy."

"Though thou get this, there is yet that which thou wilt not get. The harp of Teirtu to play to us that night. [89] When a man desires that it should play, it does so of itself, and when he desires that it should cease, it ceases. And this he will not give of his own free will, and thou wilt not be able to compel him."

"It will be easy for me to compass this, although thou mayest think that it will not be easy."

"Though thou get this, there is yet that which thou wilt not get. The cauldron of Diwrnach Wyddel, the steward of Odgar the son of Aedd, king of Ireland, to boil the meat for thy marriage feast."

"It will be easy for me to compass this, although thou mayest think that it will not be easy."

"Though thou get this, there is yet that which thou wilt not get. It is needful for me to wash my head, and shave my beard, and I require the tusk of Yskithyrwyn Benbaedd to shave myself withal, neither shall I profit by its use if it be not plucked alive out of his head."

"It will be easy for me to compass this, although thou mayest think that it will not be easy."

"Though thou get this, there is yet that which thou wilt not get. There is no one in the world that can pluck it out of his head except Odgar the son of Aedd, king of Ireland."

"It will be easy for me to compass this."

"Though thou get this, there is yet that which thou wilt not get. I will not trust any one to keep the tusk except Gado of North Britain. Now the threescore Cantrevs of North Britain are under his sway, and of his own free will he will not come out of his kingdom, and thou wilt not be able to compel him."

"It will be easy for me to compass this, although thou mayest think that it wilt not be easy."

"Though thou get this, there is yet that which thou wilt not get. I must spread out my hair in order to shave it, and it will never be spread out unless I have the blood of the jet black sorceress, the daughter of the pure white sorceress, from Pen Nant Govid, on the confines of Hell."

"It will be easy for me to compass this, although thou mayest think that it will not be easy."

"Though thou get this, there is yet that which thou wilt not get. I will not have the blood unless I have it warm, and no vessels will keep warm the liquid that is put therein except the bottles of Gwyddolwyn Gorr, which preserve the heat of the liquor that is put into them in the east, until they arrive at the west. And he will not give them of his own free will, and thou wilt not be able to compel him."

"It will be easy for me to compass this, although thou mayest think that it will not be easy."

"Though thou get this, there is yet that which thou wilt not get. Some will desire fresh milk, and it will not be possible to have fresh milk for all, unless we have the bottles of Rhinnon Rhin Barnawd, wherein no liquor ever turns sour. And he will not give them of his own free will, and thou wilt not be able to compel him."

"It will be easy for me to compass this, although thou mayest think that it will not be easy."

"Though thou get this, there is yet that which thou wilt not get. Throughout the world there is not a comb or scissors with which I can arrange my hair, on account of its rankness, except the comb and scissors that are between the two ears of Twrch Trwyth, the son of Prince Tared. He will not give them of his own free will, and thou wilt not be able to compel him."

"It will be easy for me to compass this, although thou mayest think that it will not be easy."

"Though thou get this, there is yet that which thou wilt not get. It will not be possible to hunt Twrch Trwyth without Drudwyn, the whelp of Greid, the son of Eri."

"It will be easy for me to compass this, although thou mayest think that it will not be easy."

"Though thou get this, there is yet that which thou wilt not get. Throughout the world there is not a leash that can hold him, except the leash of Cwrs Cant Ewin."

"It will be easy for me to compass this, although thou mayest think that it will not be easy."

"Though thou get this, there is yet that which thou wilt not get. Throughout the world there is no collar that wilt hold the leash except the collar of Canhastyr Canllaw."

"It will be easy for me to compass this, although thou mayest think that it will not be easy."

"Though thou get this, there is yet that which thou wilt not get. The chain of Kilydd Canhastyr to fasten the collar to the leash."

"It will be easy for me to compass this, although thou mayest think that it will not be easy."

"Though thou get this, there is yet that which thou wilt not get. Throughout the world there is not a huntsman who can hunt with this dog, except Mabon the son of Modron. He was taken from his mother when three nights old, and it is not known where he now is, nor whether he is living or dead."

"It will be easy for me to compass this, although thou mayest think that it will not be easy."

"Though thou get this, there is yet that which thou wilt not get. Gwynn Mygdwn, the horse of Gweddw that is as swift as the wave, to carry Mabon the son of Modron to hunt the Boar Trwyth. He will not give him of his own free will, and thou wilt not be able to compel him."

"It will be easy for me to compass this, although thou mayest think that it will not be easy."

"Though thou get this, there is yet that which thou wilt not get. Thou wilt not get Mabon, for it is not known where he is, unless thou find Eidoel, his kinsman in blood, the son of Aer. For it would be useless to seek for him. He is his cousin."

"It will be easy for me to compass this, although thou mayest think that it will not be easy."

"Though thou get this, there is yet that which thou wilt not get. Garselit the Gwyddelian [92] is the chief huntsman of Ireland; the Twrch Trwyth can never be hunted without him."

"It will be easy for me to compass this, although thou mayest think that it will not be easy."

"Though thou get this, there is yet that which thou wilt not get. A leash made from the beard of Dissull Varvawc, for that is the only one that can hold those two cubs. And the leash will be of no avail unless it be plucked from his beard while he is alive, and twitched out with wooden tweezers. While he lives he will not suffer this to be done to him, and the leash will be of no use should he be dead, because it will be brittle."

"It will be easy for me to compass this, although thou mayest think that it will not be easy."

"Though thou get this, there is yet that which thou wilt not get. Throughout the world there is no huntsman that can hold those two whelps, except Kynedyr Wyllt, the son of Hettwn Glafyrawc; he is nine times more wild than the wildest beast upon the mountains. Him wilt thou never get, neither wilt thou ever get my daughter."

"It will be easy for me to compass this, although thou mayest think that it will not be easy."

"Though thou get this, there is yet that which thou wilt not get. It is not possible to hunt the Boar Trwyth without Gwynn the son of Nudd, whom God has placed over the brood of devils in Annwn, lest they should destroy the present race. He will never be spared thence."

"It will be easy for me to compass this, although thou mayest think that it will not be easy."

"Though thou get this, there is yet that which thou wilt not get. There is not a horse in the world that can carry Gwynn to hunt the Twrch Trwyth, except Du, the horse of Mor of Oerveddawg." [93]

"It will be easy for me to compass this, although thou mayest think that it will not be easy."

"Though thou get this, there is yet that which thou wilt not get. Until Gilennhin the king of France shall come, the Twrch Trwyth cannot be hunted. It will be unseemly for him to leave his kingdom for thy sake, and he will never come hither."

"It will be easy for me to compass this, although thou mayest think that it will not be easy."

"Though thou get this, there is yet that which thou wilt not get. The Twrch Trwyth can never be hunted without the son of Alun Dyved; he is well skilled in letting loose the dogs."

"It will be easy for me to compass this, although thou mayest think that it will not be easy."

"Though thou get this, there is yet that which thou wilt not get. The Twrch Trwyth cannot be hunted unless thou get Aned and Aethlem. They are as swift as the gale of wind, and they were never let loose upon a beast that they did not kill him."

"It will be easy for me to compass this, although thou mayest think that it will not be easy."

"Though thou get this, there is yet that which thou wilt not get; Arthur and his companions to hunt the Twrch Trwyth. He is a mighty man, and he will not come for thee, neither wilt thou be able to compel him."

"It will be easy for me to compass this, although thou mayest think that it will not be easy."

"Though thou get this, there is yet that which thou wilt not get. The Twrch Trwyth cannot be hunted unless thou get Bwlch, and Kyfwlch, [and Sefwlch,] the grandsons of Cleddyf Difwlch. Their three shields are three gleaming glitterers. Their three spears are three pointed piercers. Their three swords are three griding gashers, Glas, Glessic, and Clersag. Their three dogs, Call, Cuall, and Cavall, Their three horses, Hwyrdydwg, and Drwgdydwg, and Llwyrdydwg. Their three wives, Och, and Geram, and Diaspad. Their three grandchildren, Lluched, and Vyned, and Eissiwed. Their three daughters, Drwg, and Gwaeth, and Gwaethav Oil. Their three handmaids, [Eheubryd, the daughter of Kyfwlch; Gorasgwrn, the daughter of Nerth; and Gwaedan, the daughter of Kynvelyn.] These three men shall sound the horn, and all the others shall shout, so that all will think that the sky is falling to the earth."

"It will be easy for me to compass this, although thou mayest think that it will not be easy."

"Though thou get this, there is yet that which thou wilt not get. The sword of Gwrnach the Giant; he will never be slain except therewith. Of his own free will he will not give it, either for a price or as a gift, and thou wilt never be able to compel him."

"It will be easy for me to compass this, although thou mayest think that it will not be easy."

"Though thou get this, there is yet that which thou wilt not get. Difficulties shall thou meet with, and nights without sleep, in seeking this, and if thou obtain it not, neither shalt thou obtain my daughter."

"Horses shall I have, and chivalry; and my lord and kinsman Arthur will obtain for me all these things. And I shall gain thy daughter, and thou shalt lose thy life."

"Go forward. And thou shalt not be chargeable for food or raiment for my daughter while thou art seeking these things; and when thou hast compassed all these marvels, thou shalt have my daughter for thy wife."

* * * * *

All that day they journeyed until the evening, and then they beheld a vast castle, which was the largest in the world. And lo, a black man, huger than three of the men of this world, came out from the castle. And they spoke unto him, "Whence comest them, O man?" "From the castle which you see yonder." "Whose castle is that?" asked they. "Stupid are ye truly, O men. There is no one in the world that does not know to whom this castle belongs. It is the castle of Gwrnach the Giant." "What treatment is there for guests and strangers that alight in that castle?" "Oh! chieftain, Heaven protect thee. No guest ever returned thence alive, and no one may enter therein unless he brings with him his craft."

Then they proceeded towards the gate. Said Gwrhyr Gwalstawd Ieithoedd, "Is there a porter?" "There is. And thou, if thy tongue be not mute in thy head, wherefore dost thou call?" "Open the gate." "I will not open it." "Wherefore wilt thou not?" "The knife is in the meat, and the drink is in the horn, and there is revelry in the hall of Gwrnach the Giant, and except for a craftsman who brings his craft, the gate will not be opened to-night." "Verily, porter," then said Kai, "my craft bring I with me." "What is thy craft?" "The best burnisher of swords am I in the world." "I will go and tell this unto Gwrnach the Giant, and I will bring thee an answer."

So the porter went in, and Gwrnach said to him, "Hast thou any news from the gate?" "I have. There is a party at the door of the gate who desire to come in." "Didst thou enquire of them if they possessed any art?" "I did enquire," said he, "and one told me that he was well skilled in the burnishing of swords." "We have need of him then. For some time have I sought for some one to polish my sword, and could find no one. Let this man enter, since he brings with him his craft."

The porter thereupon returned, and opened the gate. And Kai went in by himself, and he saluted Gwrnach the Giant. And a chair was placed for him opposite to Gwrnach. And Gwrnach said to him, "Oh man! is it true that is reported of thee that thou knowest how to burnish swords?" "I know full well how to do so," answered Kai. Then was the sword of Gwrnach brought to him. And Kai took a blue whetstone from under his arm, and asked him whether he would have it burnished white or blue. "Do with it as it seems good to thee, and as thou wouldest if it were thine own." Then Kai polished one half of the blade and put it in his hand. "Will this please thee?" asked he. "I would rather than all that is in my dominions that the whole of it were like unto this. It is a marvel to me that such a man as thou should be without a companion." "Oh! noble sir, I have a companion, albeit he is not skilled in this art." "Who may he be?" "Let the porter go forth, and I will tell him whereby he may know him. The head of his lance will leave its shaft, and draw blood from the wind, and will descend upon its shaft again." Then the gate was opened, and Bedwyr entered. And Kai said, "Bedwyr is very skilful, although he knows not this art."

And there was much discourse among those who were without, because that Kai and Bedwyr had gone in. And a young man who was with them, the only son of Custennin the herdsman, got in also. And he caused all his companions to keep close to him as he passed the three wards, and until he came into the midst of the castle. [98a] And his companions said unto the son of Custennin, "Thou hast done this! Thou art the best of all men." And thenceforth he was called Goreu, the son of Custennin. Then they dispersed to their lodgings, that they might slay those who lodged therein, unknown to the Giant.

The sword was now polished, and Kai gave it unto the hand of Gwrnach the Giant, to see if he were pleased with his work. And the Giant said, "The work is good, I am content therewith." Said Kai, "It is thy scabbard that hath rusted thy sword; give it to me that I may take out the wooden sides of it, and put in new ones." And he took the scabbard from him, and the sword in the other hand. And he came and stood over against the Giant, as if he would have put the sword into the scabbard; and with it he struck at the head of the Giant, and cut off his head at one blow. Then they despoiled the castle, and took from it what goods and jewels they would. And again on the same day, at the beginning of the year, they came to Arthur's Court, bearing with them the sword of Gwrnach the Giant.

Now when they had told Arthur how they had sped, Arthur said, "Which of these marvels will it be best for us to seek first?" "It will be best," said they, "to seek Mabon the son of Modron; and he will not be found unless we first find Eidoel, the son of Aer, his kinsman." Then Arthur rose up, and the warriors of the Islands of Britain with him, to seek for Eidoel; and they proceeded until they came before the Castle of Glivi, [98b] where Eidoel was imprisoned. Glivi [99a] stood on the summit of his Castle, and he said, "Arthur, what requirest thou of me, since nothing remains to me in this fortress, and I have neither joy nor pleasure in it; neither wheat nor oats? Seek not therefore to do me harm." Said Arthur, "Not to injure thee came I hither, but to seek for the prisoner that is with thee." "I will give thee my prisoner, though I had not thought to give him up to any one; and therewith shall thou have my support and my aid."

His followers said unto Arthur, "Lord, go thou home, thou canst not proceed with thy host in quest of such small adventures as these." Then said Arthur, "It were well for thee, Gwrhyr Gwalstawd Iethoedd, to go upon this quest, for thou knowest all languages, and art familiar with [99b] those of the birds and the beasts. Thou Eidoel oughtest likewise to go with my men in search of thy cousin. And as for you, Kai and Bedwyr, I have hope of whatever adventure ye are in quest of, that ye will achieve it. Achieve ye this adventure for me."

They went forward until they came to the Ousel of Cilgwri. And Gwrhyr adjured her for the sake of Heaven, saying, "Tell me if thou knowest aught of Mabon the son of Modron, who was taken when three nights old from between his mother and the wall." And the Ousel answered, "When I first came here, there was a smith's anvil in this place, and I was then a young bird; and from that time no work has been done upon it, save the pecking of my beak every evening, and now there is not so much as the size of a nut remaining thereof; yet the vengeance of Heaven be upon me, if during all that time I have ever heard of the man for whom you enquire. Nevertheless I will do that which is right, and that which it is fitting that I should do for an embassy from Arthur. There is a race of animals who were formed before me, and I will be your guide to them."

So they proceeded to the place where was the Stag of Redynvre. "Stag of Redynvre, behold we are come to thee, an embassy from Arthur, for we have not heard of any animal older than thou. Say, knowest thou aught of Mabon the son of Modron, who was taken from his mother when three nights old?" The Stag said, "When first I came hither, there was a plain all around me, without any trees save one oak sapling, [100] which grew up to be an oak with an hundred branches. And that oak has since perished, so that now nothing remains of it but the withered stump; and from that day to this I have been here, yet have I never heard of the man for whom you enquire. Nevertheless, being an embassy from Arthur, I will be your guide to the place where there is an animal which was formed before I was."

So they proceeded to the place where was the Owl of Cwm Cawlwyd. "Owl of Cwm Cawlwyd, here is an embassy from Arthur; knowest thou aught of Mabon the son of Modron, who was taken after three nights from his mother?" "If I knew I would tell you. When first I came hither, the wide valley you see was a wooded glen. And a race of men came and rooted it up. And there grew there a second wood; and this wood is the third. My wings, are they not withered stumps? Yet all this time, even until to-day, I have never heard of the man for whom you enquire. Nevertheless, I will be the guide of Arthur's embassy until you come to the place where is the oldest animal in this world, and the one that has travelled most, the Eagle of Gwern Abwy."

Gwrhyr said, "Eagle of Gwern Abwy, we have come to thee an embassy from Arthur, to ask thee if thou knowest aught of Mabon the son of Modron, who was taken from his mother when he was three nights old." The Eagle said, "I have been here for a great space of time, and when I first came hither there was a rock here, from the top of which I pecked at the stars every evening; and now it is not so much as a span high. From that day to this I have been here, and I have never heard of the man for whom you enquire, except once when I went in search of food as far as Llyn Llyw. And when I came there, I struck my talons into a salmon, thinking he would serve me as food for a long time. But he drew me into the deep, and I was scarcely able to escape from him. After that I went with my whole kindred to attack him, and to try to destroy him, but he sent messengers, and made peace with me; and came and besought me to take fifty fish spears out of his back. Unless he know something of him whom you seek, I cannot tell who may. However, I will guide you to the place where he is."

So they went thither; and the Eagle said, "Salmon of Llyn Llyw, I have come to thee with an embassy from Arthur, to ask thee if thou knowest aught concerning Mabon the son of Modron, who was taken away at three nights old from his mother." "As much as I know I will tell thee. With every tide I go along the river upwards, until I come near to the walls of Gloucester, and there have I found such wrong as I never found elsewhere; and to the end that ye may give credence thereto, let one of you go thither upon each of my two shoulders." So Kai and Gwrhyr Gwalstawd Ieithoedd went upon the two shoulders of the salmon, and they proceeded until they came unto the wall of the prison, and they heard a great wailing and lamenting from the dungeon. [102] Said Gwrhyr, "Who is it that laments in this house of stone?" "Alas, there is reason enough for whoever is here to lament. It is Mabon the son of Modron who is here imprisoned, and no imprisonment was ever so grievous as mine, neither that of Lludd Llaw Ereint, nor that of Greid the son of Eri." "Hast thou hope of being released for gold, or for silver, or for any gifts of wealth, or through battle and fighting?" "By fighting will whatever I may gain be obtained."

Then they went thence, and returned to Arthur, and they told him where Mabon the son of Modron was imprisoned. And Arthur summoned the warriors of the Island, and they journeyed as far as Gloucester, to the place where Mabon was in prison. Kai and Bedwyr went upon the shoulders of the fish, whilst the warriors of Arthur attacked the castle. And Kai broke through the wall into the dungeon, and brought away the prisoner upon his back, whilst the fight was going on between the warriors. And Arthur returned home, and Mabon with him at liberty.

* * * * *

Said Arthur, "Which of the marvels will it be best for us now to seek first?" "It will be best to seek for the two cubs of Gast Rhymhi." "Is it known," said Arthur, "where she is?" "She is in Aber Deu Gleddyf," said one. Then Arthur went to the house of Tringad, in Aber Cleddyf, and he enquired of him whether he had heard of her there. "In what form may she be?" "She is in the form of a she wolf," said he, "and with her there are two cubs." "She has often slain my herds, and she is there below in a cave in Aber Cleddyf."

So Arthur went in his ship Prydwen by sea, and the others went by land, to hunt her. And they surrounded her and her two cubs, and God did change them again for Arthur into their own form. And the host of Arthur dispersed themselves into parties of one and two.

* * * * *

On a certain day, as Gwythyr the son of Greidawl was walking over a mountain, he heard a wailing and a grievous cry. And when he heard it, [103] he sprung forward, and went towards it. And when he came there, he drew his sword, and smote off an ant-hill close to the earth, whereby it escaped being burned in the fire. And the ants said to him, "Receive from us the blessing of Heaven, and that which no man can give we will give thee." Then they fetched the nine bushels of flax-seed which Yspaddaden Penkawr had required of Kilhwch, and they brought the full measure, without lacking any, except one flax-seed, and that the lame pismire brought in before night.

* * * * *

As Kai and Bedwyr sat on a beacon carn on the summit of Plinlimmon, in the highest wind that ever was in the world, they looked around them, and saw a great smoke towards the south, afar off, which did not bend with the wind. Then said Kai, "By the hand of my friend, behold, yonder is the fire of a robber!" Then they hastened towards the smoke, and they came so near to it, that they could see Dillus Varvawc scorching a wild Boar. "Behold, yonder is the greatest robber that ever fled from Arthur," said Bedwyr unto Kai. "Dost thou know him?" "I do know him," answered Kai, "he is Dillus Varvawc, and no leash in the world will be able to hold Drudwyn, the cub of Greid the son of Eri, save a leash made from the beard of him thou seest yonder. And that even will be useless, unless his beard be plucked alive with wooden tweezers; for if dead, it will be brittle." "What thinkest thou that we should do concerning this?" said Bedwyr. "Let us suffer him," said Kai, "to eat as much as he will of the meat, and after that he will fall asleep." And during that time they employed themselves in making the wooden tweezers. And when Kai knew certainly that he was asleep, he made a pit under his feet, the largest in the world, and he struck him a violent blow, and squeezed him into the pit. And there they twitched out his beard completely with the wooden tweezers; and after that they slew him altogether.

And from thence they both went to Gelli Wic, in Cornwall, and took the leash made of Dillus Varvawc's beard with them, and they gave it unto Arthur's hand.

Then Arthur composed this Englyn,

> Kai made a leash
> Of Dillus son of Eurei's beard.
> Were he alive, thy death he'd be.

And thereupon Kai was wroth, so that the warriors of the Island could scarcely make peace between Kai and Arthur. And thenceforth, neither in Arthur's troubles, nor for the slaying of his men, would Kai come forward to his aid for ever after.

* * * * *

Said Arthur, "Which of the marvels is it best for us now to seek?" "It is best for us to seek Drudwyn, the cub of Greid, the son of Eri."

A little while before this, Creiddylad, the daughter of Lludd Llaw Ereint, and Gwythyr the son of Greidawl, were betrothed. And before she had become his bride, Gwyn ap Nudd came, and carried her away by force; and Gwythyr the son of Greidawl gathered his host together, and went to fight with Gwyn ap Nudd. But Gwyn overcame him, and captured Greid the son of Eri, and Glinneu the son of Taran and Gwrgwst Ledlwm, and Dynvarth [105] his son. And he captured Penn the son of Nethawg, and Nwython, and Kyledyr Wyllt his son. And they slew Nwython, and took out his heart, and constrained Kyledyr to eat the heart of his father. And therefrom Kyledyr became mad. When Arthur heard of this, he went to the North, and summoned Gwyn ap Nudd before him, and set free the nobles whom he had put in prison, and made peace between Gwyn ap Nudd and Gwythyr the son of Greidawl. And this was the peace that was made: that the maiden should remain in her father's house, without advantage to either of them, and that Gwyn ap Nudd and Gwythyr the son of Greidawl should fight for her every first of May, from thenceforth until the day of doom, and that whichever of them should then be conqueror should have the maiden.

And when Arthur had thus reconciled these chieftains, he obtained Mygdwn, Gweddw's horse, and the leash of Cwrs Cant Ewin.

And after that Arthur went into Armorica, and with him Mabon the son of Mellt, and Gware Gwallt Euryn, to seek the two dogs of Glythmyr Ledewic. And when he had got them, he went to the West of Ireland, in search of Gwrgi Severi; and Odgar the son of Aedd, king of Ireland, went with him. And thence went Arthur into the North, and captured Kyledyr Wyllt; and he went after Yskithyrwyn Penbaedd. And Mabon the son of Mellt came with the two dogs of Glythmyr Ledewic in his hand, and Drudwyn, the cub of Greid the son of Eri. And Arthur went himself to the chase, leading his own dog Cavall. And Kaw, of North Britain, mounted Arthur's mare Llamrei, and was first in the attack. Then Kaw, of North Britain, wielded a mighty axe, and absolutely daring he came valiantly up to the Boar, and clave his head in twain. And Kaw took away the tusk. Now the Boar was not slain by the dogs that Yspaddaden had mentioned, but by Cavall, Arthur's own dog.

And after Yskithyrwyn Penbaedd was killed, Arthur and his host departed to Gelli Wic in Cornwall. And thence he sent Menw the son of Teirgwaedd to see if the precious things were between the two ears of Twrch Trwyth, since it were useless to encounter him if they were not there. Albeit it was certain where he was, for he had laid waste the third part of Ireland. And Menw went to seek for him, and he met with him in Ireland, in Esgeir Oervel. And Menw took the form of a bird; and he descended upon the top of his lair, and strove to snatch away one of the precious things from him, but he carried away nothing but one of his bristles. And the boar rose up angrily and shook himself so that some of his venom fell upon Menw, and he was never well from that day forward.

After this Arthur sent an embassy to Odgar, the son of Aedd, king of Ireland, to ask for the Cauldron of Diwrnach Wyddel, his purveyor. And Odgar commanded him to give it. But Diwrnach said, "Heaven is my witness, if it would avail him anything even to look at it, he should not do so." And the embassy of Arthur returned from Ireland with this denial. And Arthur set forward with a small retinue, and entered into Prydwen, his ship, and went over to Ireland. And they proceeded into the house of Diwrnach Wyddel. And the hosts of Odgar saw their strength. When they had eaten and drank as much as they desired, Arthur demanded to have the cauldron. And he answered, "If I would have given it to any one, I would have given it at the word of Odgar, king of Ireland."

When he had given them this denial, Bedwyr arose and seized hold of the cauldron, and placed it upon the back of Hygwyd, Arthur's servant, who was brother, by the mother's side, to Arthur's servant, Cachamwri. His office was always to carry Arthur's cauldron, and to place fire under it. And Llenlleawg Wyddel seized Caledvwlch, and brandished it. And they slew Diwrnach Wyddel and his company. Then came the Irish, [108a] and fought with them. And when he had put them to flight, Arthur with his men went forward to the ship, carrying away the cauldron full of Irish money. [108b] And he disembarked at the house of Llwydden [108c] the son of Kelcoed, at Forth Kerddin in Dyved. And there is the measure of the cauldron.

Then Arthur summoned unto him all the warriors that were in the three Islands of Britain, and in the three Islands adjacent, and all that were in France and in Armorica, in Normandy and in the Summer Country, and all that were chosen footmen and valiant horsemen. And with all these, he went into Ireland. And in Ireland there was great fear and terror concerning him. And when Arthur had landed in the country, there came unto him the saints of Ireland and besought his protection. And he granted his protection unto them, and they gave him their blessing. Then the men of Ireland came unto Arthur, and brought him provisions. And Arthur went as far as Esgeir Oervel in Ireland, to the place where the Boar Trwyth was with his seven young pigs. And the dogs were let loose upon him from all sides. That day until evening, the Irish fought with him, nevertheless he laid waste the fifth part of Ireland. And on the day following the household of Arthur fought with him, and they were worsted by him, and got no advantage. And the third day Arthur himself encountered him, and he fought with him nine nights and nine days without so much as killing even one little pig. [109] The warriors enquired of Arthur, what was the origin of that swine; and he told them that he was once a king, and that God had transformed him into a swine for his sins.

Then Arthur sent Gwrhyr Gwalstawt Ieithoedd, to endeavour to speak with him. And Gwrhyr assumed the form of a bird, and alighted upon the top of the lair, where he was with the seven young pigs. And Gwrhyr Gwalstawt Ieithoedd asked him, "By him who turned you into this form, if you can speak, let some one of you, I beseech you, come and talk with Arthur." Grugyn Gwrych Ereint made answer to him. (Now his bristles were like silver wire, and whether he went through the wood or through the plain, he was to be traced by the glittering of his bristles.) And this was the answer that Grugyn made, "By him who turned us into this form we will not do so, and we will not speak with Arthur. That we have been transformed thus is enough for us to suffer, without your coming here to fight with us." "I will tell you. Arthur comes but to fight for the comb, and the razor, and the scissors, which are between the two ears of Twrch Trwyth." Said Grugyn, "Except he first take his life, he will never have those precious things. And to-morrow morning we will rise up hence, and we will go into Arthur's country, and there will we do all the mischief that we can."

So they set forth through the sea towards Wales. And Arthur and his hosts, and his horses and his dogs, entered Prydwen, that they might encounter them without delay. Twrch Trwyth landed in Porth Cleis in Dyved, and the [110] came to Mynyw. The next day it was told to Arthur, that they had gone by, and he overtook them, as they were killing the cattle of Kynnwas Kwrr y Vagyl, having slain all that were at Aber Gleddyf, of man and beast, before the coming of Arthur.

Now when Arthur approached, Twrch Trwyth went on as far as Preseleu, and Arthur and his hosts followed him thither, and Arthur sent men to hunt him; Eli and Trachmyr, leading Drutwyn the whelp of Greid, the son of Eri, and Gwarthegyd the son of Kaw, in another quarter, with the two dogs of Glythmyr Ledewig, and Bedwyr leading Cavall, Arthur's own dog. And all the warriors ranged themselves around the Nyver. And there came there the three sons of Cleddyf Divwlch, men who had gained much fame at the slaying of Yskithyrwyn Penbaedd; and they went on from Glyn Nyver, and came to Cwm Kerwyn.

And there Twrch Trwyth made a stand, and slew four of Arthur's champions, Gwarthegyd the son of Kaw, and Tarawc of Allt Clwyd, and Rheidwn the son of Eli Atver, and Iscovan Hael. And after he had slain these men, he made a second stand in the same place. And there he slew Gwydre the son of Arthur, and Garselit Wyddel, and Glew the son of Ysgawd, and Iscawn the son of Panon; and there he himself was wounded.

And the next morning before it was day, some of the men came up with him. And he slew Huandaw, and Gogigwr, and Penpingon, three attendants upon Glewlwyd Gavaelvawr, so that Heaven knows he had not an attendant remaining, excepting only Llaesgevyn, a man from whom no one ever derived any good. And together with these, he slew many of the men of that country, and Gwlydyn Saer, Arthur's chief Architect.

Then Arthur overtook him at Pelumyawc, and there he slew Madawc the son of Teithyon, and Gwyn the son of Tringad, the son of Neved, and Eiryawn Penllorau. Thence he went to Aberteivi, [111a] where he made another stand, and where he slew Kyflas [111b] the son of Kynan, and Gwilenhin king of France. Then he went as far as Glyn Ystu, and there the men and the dogs lost him.

Then Arthur summoned unto him Gwyn ab Nudd, and he asked him if he knew aught of Twrch Trwyth. And he said that he did not.

And all the huntsmen went to hunt the swine as far as Dyffryn Llychwr. And Grugyn Gwallt Ereint, and Llwydawg Govynnyad closed with them and killed all the huntsmen, so that there escaped but one man only. And Arthur and his hosts came to the place where Grugyn and Llwydawg were. And there he let loose the whole of the dogs upon them, and with the shout and barking that was set up, Twrch Trwyth came to their assistance.

And from the time that they came across the Irish sea, Arthur had never got sight of him until then. [111c] So he set men and dogs upon him, and thereupon he started off and went to Mynydd Amanw. And there one of his young pigs was killed. [112a] Then they set upon him life for life, and Twrch Llawin was slain, and then there was slain another of the swine, Gwys was his name. After that he went on to Dyffryn Amanw, and there Banw and Bennwig were killed. [112b] Of all his pigs there went with him alive from that place none save Grugyn Gwallt Ereint, and Llwydawg Govynnyad.

Thence he went on to Llwch Ewin, and Arthur overtook him there, and he made a stand. And there he slew Echel Forddwytwll, and Garwyli the son of Gwyddawg Gwyr, and many men and dogs likewise. And thence they went to Llwch Tawy. Grugyn Gwrych Ereint parted from them there, and went to Din Tywi. And thence he proceeded to Ceredigiawn, and Eli and Trachmyr with him, and a multitude likewise. Then he came to Garth

Gregyn, and there Llwydawg Govynnyad fought in the midst of them, and slew Rhudvyw Rhys and many others with him. Then Llwydawg went thence to Ystrad Yw, and there the men of Armorica met him, and there he slew Hirpeissawg, the king of Armorica, and Llygatrudd Emys, and Gwrbothu, Arthur's uncles, his mother's brothers, and there was he himself slain.

Twrch Trwyth went from there to between Tawy and Euyas, and Arthur summoned all Cornwall and Devon unto him, to the estuary of the Severn, and he said to the warriors of this Island, "Twrch Trwyth has slain many of my men, but, by the valour of warriors, while I live he shall not go into Cornwall. And I will not follow him any longer, but I will oppose him life to life. Do ye as ye will." And he resolved that he would send a body of knights, with the dogs of the Island, as far as Euyas, who should return thence to the Severn, and that tried warriors should traverse the Island, and force him into the Severn. And Mabon the son of Modron came up with him at the Severn, upon Gwynn Mygddon, the horse of Gweddw, and Goreu the son of Custennin, and Menw the son of Teirgwaedd; this was betwixt Llyn Lliwan and Aber Gwy. And Arthur fell upon him together with the champions of Britain. And Osla Kyllellvawr drew near, and Manawyddan the son of Llyr, and Kacmwri the servant of Arthur, and Gwyngelli, and they seized hold of him, catching him first by his feet, and plunged him in the Severn, so that it overwhelmed him. On the one side, Mabon the son of Modron spurred his steed and snatched his razor from him, and Kyledyr Wyllt came up with him on the other side, upon another steed, in the Severn, and took from him the scissors. But before they could obtain the comb, he had regained the ground with his feet, and from the moment that he reached the shore, neither dog, nor man, nor horse could overtake him until he came to Cornwall. If they had had trouble in getting the jewels from him, much more had they in seeking to save the two men from being drowned. Kacmwri, as they drew him forth, was dragged by two millstones into the deep. And as Osla Kyllellvawr was running after the Boar his knife had dropped out of the sheath, and he had lost it, and after that the sheath became full of water, and its weight drew him down into the deep, as they were drawing him forth.

Then Arthur and his hosts proceeded until they overtook the Boar in Cornwall, and the trouble which they had met with before was mere play to what they encountered in seeking the comb. But from one difficulty to another, the comb was at length obtained. And then he was hunted from Cornwall, and driven straight forward into the deep sea. And thenceforth it was never known whither he went; and Aned and Aethlem with him. Then went Arthur to Gelliwic, in Cornwall, to anoint himself, and to rest from his fatigues.

* * * * *

Said Arthur, "Is there any one of the marvels yet unobtained?" Said one of his men, "There is—the blood of the witch Orddu, the daughter of the witch Orwen, of Penn Nant Govid, on the confines of Hell." Arthur set forth towards the North, and came to the place where was the witch's cave. And Gwyn ab Nudd, and Gwythyr the son of Greidawl, counselled him to send Kacmwri, and Hygwyd his brother to fight with the witch. And as they entered the cave, the witch seized upon them, and she caught Hygwyd by the hair of his head, and threw him on the floor beneath her. And Kacmwri caught her by the hair of her head, and dragged her to the earth from off Hygwyd, but she turned again upon them both, [114] and drove them both out with kicks and with cuffs.

And Arthur was wroth at seeing his two attendants almost slain, and he sought to enter the cave; but Gwyn and Gwythyr said unto him, "It would not be fitting or seemly for us to see thee squabbling with a hag. Let Hiramren, and Hireidil go to the cave." So they went. But if great was the trouble of the two first that went, much greater was that of these two. And Heaven knows that not one of the four could move from the spot, until they placed them all upon Llamrei, Arthur's mare. And then Arthur rushed to the door of the cave, and at the door, he struck at the witch, with Carnwennan his dagger, and clove her in twain, so that she fell in two parts. And Kaw, of North Britain, took the blood of the witch and kept it.

Then Kilhwch set forward, and Goreu, the son of Custennin, with him, and as many as wished ill to Yspaddaden Penkawr. And they took the marvels with them to his Court. And Kaw of North Britain came and shaved his beard, skin and flesh, clean off to the very bone from ear to ear. "Art thou shaved, man?" said Kilhwch. "I am shaved," answered he. "Is thy daughter mine now?" "She is thine," said he, "but therefore needest thou not thank me, but Arthur who hath accomplished this for thee. By my free will thou shouldest never have had her, for with her I lose my life." Then Goreu the son of Custennin, seized him by the hair of his head, and dragged him after him to the keep, and cut off his head, and placed it on a stake on the citadel. Then they took possession of his castle, and of his treasures.

And that night Olwen became Kilhwch's bride, and she continued to be his wife as long as she lived. And the hosts of Arthur dispersed themselves, each man to his own country. And thus did Kilhwch obtain Olwen the daughter of Yspaddaden Penkawr.

THE DREAM OF MAXEN WLEDIG.

Maxen Wledig was emperor of Rome, and he was a comelier man, and a better and a wiser than any emperor that had been before him. [116] And one day he held a council of Kings, and he said to his friends, "I desire to go to-morrow to hunt." And the next day in the morning he set forth with his retinue, and came to the valley of the river that flowed towards Rome. And he hunted through the valley until mid-day. And with him also were two and thirty crowned kings, that were his vassals; not for the delight of hunting went the emperor with them, but to put himself on equal terms with those kings. [117]

And the sun was high in the sky over their heads, and the heat was great. And sleep came upon Maxen Wledig. And his attendants stood and set up their shields around him upon the shafts of their spears to protect him from the sun, and they placed a gold enamelled shield under his head, and so Maxen slept.

And he saw a dream. And this is the dream that he saw. He was journeying along the valley of the river towards its source; and he came to the highest mountain in the world. And he thought that the mountain was as high as the sky; and when he came over the mountain, it seemed to him that he went through the fairest and most level regions that man ever yet beheld, on the other side of the mountain. And he saw large and mighty rivers descending from the mountain to the sea, and towards the mouths of the rivers he proceeded. And as he journeyed thus, he came to the mouth of the largest river ever seen. And he beheld a great city at the entrance of the river, and a vast castle in the city, and he saw many high towers of various colours in the castle. And he saw a fleet at the mouth of the river, the largest ever seen. And he saw one ship among the fleet; larger was it by far, and fairer than all the others. Of such part of the ship as he could see above the water, one plank was gilded and the other silvered over. He saw a bridge of the bone of the whale from the ship to the land, and he thought that he went along the bridge and came into the ship. And a sail was hoisted on the ship, and along the sea and the ocean was it borne. Then it seemed that he came to the fairest island in the whole world, and he traversed the island from sea to sea, even to the farthest shore of the island. Valleys he saw, and steeps, and rocks of wondrous height, and rugged precipices. [118a] Never yet saw he the like. And thence he beheld an island in the sea, facing this rugged [118b] land. And between him and this island was a country of which the plain was as large as the sea, the mountain as vast as the wood. And from the mountain he saw a river that flowed through the land and fell into the sea. And at the mouth of the river, he beheld a castle, the fairest that man ever saw, and the gate of the castle was open, and he went into the castle. And in the castle he saw a fair hall of which the roof seemed to be all gold, the walls of the hall seemed to be entirely of glittering precious gems, the doors all seemed to be of gold. Golden seats he saw in the hall, and silver tables. And on a seat opposite to him, he beheld two auburn-haired youths playing at chess. He saw a silver board for the chess, and golden pieces thereon. The garments of the youths were of jet black satin, and chaplets of ruddy gold bound their hair, whereon were sparkling jewels of great price, [119] rubies, and gems, alternately with imperial stones. Buskins of new cordovan leather on their feet, fastened by slides of red gold.

And beside a pillar in the hall he saw a hoary-headed man, in a chair of ivory, with the figures of two eagles of ruddy gold thereon. Bracelets of gold were upon his arms, and many rings upon his hands, and a golden torquis about his neck; and his hair was bound with a golden diadem. He was of powerful aspect. A chessboard of gold was before him, and a rod of gold, and a steel file in his hand. And he was carving out chessmen.

And he saw a maiden sitting before him in a chair of ruddy gold. Not more easy than to gaze upon the sun when brightest, was it to look upon her by reason of her beauty. A vest of white silk was upon the maiden, with clasps of red gold at the breast; and a surcoat of gold tissue was upon her, and a frontlet of red gold upon her head, and rubies and gems were in the frontlet, alternating with pearls and imperial stones. And a girdle of ruddy gold was around her. She was the fairest sight that man ever beheld.

The maiden arose from her chair before him, and he threw his arms about the neck of the maiden, and they two sat down together in the chair of gold: and the chair was not less roomy for them both, than for the maiden alone. And as he had his arms about the maiden's neck, and his cheek by her cheek, behold, through the chafing of the dogs at their leashing, and the clashing of the shields as they struck against each other, and the beating together of the shafts of the spears, and the neighing of the horses and their prancing, the emperor awoke.

And when he awoke, nor spirit nor existence was left him, because of the maiden whom he had seen in his sleep, for the love of the maiden pervaded his whole frame. [120] Then his household spake unto him. "Lord," said they "is it not past the time for thee to take thy food?" Thereupon the emperor mounted his palfrey, the saddest man that mortal ever saw, and went forth towards Rome.

And thus he was during the space of a week. When they of the household went to drink wine and mead out of golden vessels, he went not with any of them. When they went to listen to songs and tales, he went not with them there; neither could he be persuaded to do anything but sleep. And as often as he slept, he beheld in his dreams the maiden he loved best; but except when he slept he saw nothing of her, for he knew not where in the world she was.

One day the page of the chamber spake unto him; now, although he was page of the chamber, he was king of the Romans. "Lord," said he, "all thy people revile thee." "Wherefore do they revile me?" asked the emperor. "Because they can get neither message nor answer from thee, as men should have from their lord. This is the cause why thou art spoken evil of." "Youth," said the emperor, "do thou bring unto me the wise men of Rome, and I will tell them wherefore I am sorrowful."

Then the wise men of Rome were brought to the emperor, and he spake to them. "Sages of Rome," said he, "I have seen a dream. And in the dream I beheld a maiden, and because of the maiden is there neither life, nor spirit, nor existence within me." "Lord," they answered, "since thou judgest us worthy to counsel thee, we will give thee counsel. And this is our counsel; that thou send messengers for three years to the three parts of the world, to seek for thy dream. And as thou knowest not what day or what night good news may come to thee, the hope thereof will support thee."

So the messengers journeyed for the space of a year wandering about the world, and seeking tidings concerning his dream. But when they came back at the end of the year they knew not one word more than they did the day they set forth. And then was the emperor exceeding sorrowful, for he thought that he should never have tidings of her whom best he loved.

Then spoke the king of the Romans unto the emperor. "Lord," said he, "go forth to hunt by the way that thou didst seem to go, whither it were to the east or to the west." So the emperor went forth to hunt, and he came to the bank of the river. "Behold," said he, "this is where I was when I saw the dream, and I went towards the source of the river westward."

And thereupon thirteen messengers of the emperor's set forth, and before them they saw a high mountain, which seemed to them to touch the sky. Now this was the guise in which the messengers journeyed; one sleeve was on the cap of each of them in front; as a sign that they were messengers, in order that through what hostile land soever they might pass no harm might be done them. And when they were come over this mountain they beheld vast plains, and large rivers flowing therethrough. "Behold," said they, "the land which our master saw."

And they went along the mouths of the rivers, until they came to the mighty river which they saw flowing to the sea, and the vast city, and the many-coloured high towers in the castle. They saw the largest fleet in the world, in the harbour of the river, and one ship that was larger than any of the others. "Behold again," said they, "the dream that our master saw." And in the great ship they crossed the sea, and came to the Island of Britain. And they traversed the island until they came to Snowdon. "Behold," said they, "the rugged [122] land that our master saw." And they went forward until they saw Anglesey before them, and until they saw Arvon likewise. "Behold," said they, "the land our master saw in his sleep." And they saw Aber Sain, and a castle at the mouth of the river. The portal of the castle saw they open, and into the castle they went, and they saw a hall in the castle. Then said they, "Behold the hall which he saw in his sleep."

They went into the hall, and they beheld two youths playing at chess on the golden bench. And they beheld the hoary-headed man beside the pillar, in the ivory chair, carving chessmen. And they beheld the maiden sitting on a chair of ruddy gold.

The messengers bent down upon their knees. "Empress of Rome, all hail!" "Ha, gentles," said the maiden, "ye bear the seeming of honourable men, and the badge of envoys, what mockery is this ye do to me?" "We mock thee not, lady, but the emperor of Rome hath seen thee in his sleep, and he has neither life nor spirit left because of thee. Thou shall have of us therefore the choice, lady, whether thou wilt go with us and be made empress of Rome, or that the emperor come hither and take thee for his wife?" "Ha, lords," said the maiden, "I will not deny what you say, neither will I believe it too well. If the emperor love me, let him come here to seek me."

And by day and night the messengers hied them back. And when their horses failed, they bought other fresh ones. And when they came to Rome they saluted the emperor, and asked their boon, which was given to them according as they named it. "We will be thy guides, lord," said they, "over sea and over land, to the place where is the woman whom best thou lovest, for we know her name, and her kindred, and her race."

And immediately the emperor set forth with his army. And these men were his guides. Towards the Island of Britain they went over the sea and the deep. And he conquered the Island from Beli the son of Manogan, and his sons, and drove them to the sea, and went forward even unto Arvon. And the emperor knew the land when he saw it. And when he beheld the castle of Aber Sain, "Look yonder," said he, "there is the castle wherein I saw the damsel whom I best love." And he went forward into the castle and into the hall, and there he saw Kynan the son of Eudav, and Adeon the son of Eudav, playing at chess. And he saw Eudav the son of Caradawc, sitting on a chair of ivory carving chessmen. And the maiden whom he had beheld in his sleep, he saw sitting on a chair of gold. "Empress of Rome," said he, "all hail!" And the emperor threw his arms about her neck; and that night she became his bride.

And the next day in the morning, the damsel asked her maiden portion. And he told her to name what she would, and she asked to have the Island of Britain for her father, from the Channel to the Irish Sea, together with the three adjacent islands to hold under the empress of Rome; and to have three chief castles made for her, in whatever places she might choose in the Island of Britain. And she chose to have the highest castle made at Arvon. And they brought thither earth from Rome that it might be more healthful for the emperor to sleep, and sit, and walk upon. After that the two other castles were made for her, which were Caerlleon and Caermarthen.

And one day, the emperor went to hunt at Caermarthen, and he came so far as the top of Brevi Vawr, and there the emperor pitched his tent. And that encamping place is called Cadeir Maxen, even to this day. And because that he built the castle with a myriad of men, he called it Caervyrddin. Then Helen bethought her to make high roads from one castle to another throughout the Island of Britain. And the roads were made. And for this cause are they called the roads of Helen Luyddawc, [124] that she was sprung from a native of this island, and the men of the Island of Britain would not have made these great roads [125] for any save for her.

Seven years did the emperor tarry in this Island. Now, at that time, the men of Rome had a custom that whatsoever emperor should remain in other lands more than seven years, should remain to his own overthrow, and should never return to Rome again.

So they made a new emperor. And this one wrote a letter of threat to Maxen. There was nought in the letter but only this, "If thou comest, and if thou ever comest to Rome." And even unto Caerlleon came this letter to Maxen, and these tidings. Then sent he a letter to the man who styled himself emperor in Rome. There was nought in that letter also but only this, "If I come to Rome, and if I come."

And thereupon Maxen set forth towards Rome with his army, and vanquished France and Burgundy, and every land on the way, and sat down before the city of Rome.

A year was the emperor before the city, and he was no nearer taking it than the first day. And after him there came the brothers of Helen Luyddawc from the Island of Britain, and a small host with them, and better warriors were in that small host than twice as many Romans. And the emperor was told that a host was seen, halting close to his army and encamping, and no man ever saw a fairer or better appointed host for its size, nor more handsome standards.

And Helen went to see the hosts, and she knew the standards of her brothers. Then came Kynan the son of Eudav, and Adeon the son of Eudav, to meet the emperor. And the emperor was glad because of them, and embraced them.

Then they looked at the Romans as they attacked the city. Said Kynan to his brother, "We will try to attack the city more expertly than this." So they measured by night the height of the wall, and they sent their carpenters to the wood, and a ladder was made for every four men of their number. Now when these were ready, every day at mid-day the emperors went to meat, and they ceased to fight on both sides till all had finished eating. And in the morning the men of Britain took their food, and they drank until they were invigorated. And while the two emperors were at meat, the Britons came to the city, [126a] and placed their ladders against it, and forthwith they came in through the city.

The new emperor had not time to arm himself when they fell upon him, and slew him and many others with him. And three nights and three days were they subduing the men that were in the city and taking the castle. And others of them kept the city, lest any of the host of Maxen should come therein, until they had subjected all to their will.

Then spake Maxen to Helen Luyddawc, "I marvel, lady," said he, "that thy brothers have not conquered this city for me." [126b] "Lord, emperor," she answered, "the wisest youths in the world are my brothers. Go thou thither and ask the city of them, and if it be in their possession thou shalt have it gladly." So the emperor and Helen went and demanded the city. And they told the emperor that none had taken the city, and that none could give it him, but the men of the Island of Britain. Then the gates of the city of Rome were opened, and the emperor sat on the throne and all the men of Rome submitted themselves unto him.

The emperor then said unto Kynan and Adeon, "Lords," said he, "I have now had possession of the whole of my empire. This host give I unto you to vanquish whatever region ye may desire in the world."

So they set forth and conquered lands, and castles and cities. And they slew all the men, but the women they kept alive. And thus they continued until the young men that had come with them were grown grey headed, from the length of time they were upon this conquest.

Then spoke Kynan unto Adeon his brother, "Whether wilt thou rather," said he, "tarry in this land, or go back into the land whence thou didst come forth?" Now he chose to go back to his own land and many with him. But Kynan tarried there with the other part, and dwelt there.

And they took counsel and cut out the tongues of the women, lest they should corrupt their speech. And because of the silence of the women from their own speech, the men of Armorica are called Britons. From that time there came frequently, and still comes, that language from the Island of Britain.

And this tale is called the Dream of Maxen Wledig, emperor of Rome. And here it ends.

Footnotes:

[7a] Add "successively."

[7b] And he summoned to him.

[10] Add "bespattered."

[11] And it may be that I shall have as much entertainment on account of the hunting as they.

[15] Good Sir.

[17] There.

[19] And his words reached Geraint.

[22] As thou art impartial concerning the question of right between us.

[27] More probably "though." The ambiguity of the original would be best expressed by "while."

[36a] "Lest he should be overtaken by a piteous death."

[36b] "Thine I do not consider a protection, nor thy warning a warning."

[38] "Wilt thou not at last be silent? Thy protection do I not consider such."

[39] "I declare to Heaven," said he, "that thy protection I do not regard as such. Hold thy peace, at last."

[40] He spoke not a word, being angry.

[47a] "Do thou not go to his land beyond the bridge."

[47b] "I will go my way in spite of the one thou speakest of."

[48a] In a very rough and bitter manner.

[48b] Gereint took the road that he had meant to take; it was not the road that led to the town from the bridge that he took, but the road that led to the ground that was hard, and rugged, and high, and ridgy.

[49] But it was unfair for Gereint to have to fight him, so small was he, and so difficult to take aim at, and so hard were the blows he gave. And they did not end that part of their fight until their horses fell down on their knees.

[53] "To complete thy death."

[64] And what she did was to call her tutor to her, and she commanded him to dress her grave every year in such a way that nothing would grow on it.

[66] And there were two silver spears, sharpened, in his hand. A prince's glaive was in his hand, a cubit from hilt to edge, that would draw blood from the wind; swifter was it than.

[67] Yes. And as for thee, thy head is not under thy control; curt is thy greeting.

[70a] Carnwenhan.

[70b] Dress.

[71a] Galldovydd.

[71b] Cnychwr.

[71c] And Adwy.

[71d] Annwas.

[71e] Sinoit.

[72a] Ysperin.

[72b] Erinit.

[74a] Llenuleawc.

[74b] Gwrdival.

[74c] Kai was said to be his son.

[75a] Add, "And from him is Paris named."

[75b] Gweir, son of Cadellin Talaryant (Cadellin of the silver brow).

[76a] His flat breast was ruddy.

[77a] Hwyrdyddwc, Drwgdyddwc, and Llwyrdyddwc.

[77b] Cethtrwm.

[78a] Gweirdathar Wenidawc.

[78b] Canhwch.

[78c] Arwy.

[81a] "We all of us will come there," said Kai.

[81b] This dialogue consists of a series of repartees, with a play upon words which it is impossible to follow in the translation.

[82] "Oh man, since the sea does not allow a beautiful dead man in it, show me that dead body." "Oh woman, the one to whom the dead body belongs thou wilt see here this evening."

[84a] "I promise all this, and will obtain it," said he.

[84b] "Where are my bad servants and my knaves?"

[85a] Knee-pan.

[87] The two oxen of Gwlwlwyd Wineu.

[89] The harp of Teirtu to console me that night.

[92] Garselit Wyddel.

[93] Moro Oerveddawc.

[98a] And what he and his companions with him did was this—they crossed the three wards until he was within the fortress.

[98b] Glini.

[99a] Glini.

[99b] Add "some of."

[100] There was but one horn on each side of my head, and there were no trees here except one oak sapling.

[102] And they proceeded until they came to the wall opposite to where the prisoner was, where they heard lamentations and groaning on the other side of the wall.

[103] And it was piteous to hear them. And he hastened to the place.

[105] Dyvnarth.

[108a] Hosts of Ireland.

[108b] And when all the hosts had fled, Arthur and his men went to their ship in their sight, carrying with them the cauldron full of Irish money.

[108c] Llwyddeu.

[109] And he only killed one of his young pigs.

[110] Add "same night Arthur."

[111a] Aber Tywi.

[111b] Kynlas.

[111c] And ever since they had crossed the Irish Sea, he had not appeared to them until then.

[112a] And there was killed a young boar from among his pigs.

[112b] And there was killed a young boar and a young sow.

[114] But she turned again upon Kacmwri; she beat both men soundly, disarmed them, and drove them out.

[116] Maxen Wledig was an emperor at Rome. And the comeliest man was he, and the wisest, and the one that was most fit to be an emperor, of all that had been before him.

[117] Not for the delight of hunting went the emperor so far as that, but to make himself such a man that he would be lord over those kings.

[118a] Valleys he saw, and precipices, and wondrous high rocks, and a rugged, waterless land.

[118b] Barren.

[119] Sparkling jewels laboriously wrought.

[120] There was no joint of his bones, or cavity of his nails, not to speak of anything larger than these, that was not full of the maiden's love.

[122] Waterless.

[124] Helen of the Legions.

[125] Legions.

[126a] Over the wall into the city.

[126b] That it was not for me that thy brothers conquered the city.